TURNING FINANCIAL OBSTACLES INTO OPPORTUNITIES

WALTHER P. KALLESTAD

FOREWORD BY ROBERT SCHULLER
INTRODUCTION BY LYLE SCHALLER

TURNING
FINANCIAL
OBSTACLES
INTO
OPPORTUNITIES

BY
WALTHER P. KALLESTAD

PRINCE OF PEACE PUBLISHING
Burnsville, Minnesota 55337

Library of Congress Catalog Card Number
Kallestad, Walther P., 1948-
        Turning financial obstacles into opportunities.

        1. Church finance.   2. Finance, Personal—
Religious aspects—Christianity.   3. Kallestad, Walther P.,
1948-   I. Title.
BV770.K35   1987   254.8   87-3361
ISBN 0-933173-12-1

Printed in the United States of America

Dedication

With great love, joy and enthusiasm,
I dedicate this book to my beloved family of
Community Church of Joy
without whose friendship and partnership in mission
I could not have written
what you are about to read.

Obstacles can become a magnet that draws us closer to God and to one another, producing tougher faith and a more tender heart. It is easy to see obstacles as an enemy to opportunity. However, obstacles placed in the hands of God can become a friend of opportunity. Obstacles cause us to think more deeply than we have ever thought before. They also cause us to feel more compassionately than perhaps we have ever felt before. One person said about obstacles:

Looking back, it seems to me
All the obstacles which had to be,
Left me when the struggle was o'er
Richer than I'd been before.

My fervent prayer and desire is that this book will help you take your obstacles, particularly your financial obstacles, and with God's power, turn them into opportunities. The great transforming miracle of turning your financial obstacles into opportunities can transpire just as the psalmist predicted: "The Lord will perfect the things that concern me."

I want to write a special note of thanks to those who worked so closely with me throughout the entire process of writing this book. Thank you, Ms. Helen Wilkman, for your long hours of typing, re-typing and reworking the manuscript. Thank you, Dr. Gary Smalley, for the hours of working face to face in developing each chapter into a more helpful gift. Thank you, Dr. Mervin Thompson, for your encouragement to grow toward excellence in communicating the "good news of Jesus Christ." A special thank you to Dr. Robert Schuller and Dr. Lyle Schaller for your great support and inspiration. Finally, I want to thank my publisher, Wayne Skaff, for believing in me enough to be willing to publish my first book.

Now, as you begin, may you always be aware of how much God loves and cherishes you.

Walther P. Kallestad

FOREWORD

by Robert H. Schuller

The first time I met Walt Kallestad, we saw God turn an obstacle into an opportunity!

It was 1975 and Walt was part of the Institute for Successful Church Leadership here in Garden Grove, California. This is a pastor's workshop that encourages ministries to "do something great for God."

Walt received a telephone call, an emergency telephone call. Their two-year-old son, Patrick, had wandered outside the home in which they were staying, and had fallen into the swimming pool. By the time Patrick was found, he was unconscious and his color was blue. They told Walt that the paramedics were rushing Patrick to the hospital.

As Walt hung up the phone, I happened to be right there. I asked Walt to tell me what had happened. Finally, I shot a prayer up to God, and said, "Lord, speak through me now."

I found myself saying, "Do you believe in miracles?"

"Yes," I heard Walt say.

Right then we prayed for a miracle for Patrick. As Walt headed for the hospital, I went into the session with the pastors and asked them to pray for Patrick.

The miracle happened! At the closing communion service of the Institute, we were able to celebrate with Walt and his family. Walt and Mary, his wife, came to the front carrying Patrick. I reached out and held Patrick high. The 500 pastors present shed tears. A miracle had transpired! We were all witnesses to God turning a life-threatening obstacle into a great opportunity.

Turning obstacles into opportunities has been the hallmark of Walt Kallestad's ministry. This book on turning financial obstacles into opportunities impresses me with the imagination, determination and enthusiasm with which financial difficulties can be overcome.

No church has a money problem. Churches have idea problems! Big, inspiring, human need-filling ideas are money-makers! Successful goals always produce their own financial support if they are widely and enthusiastically publicized. Only fear, small faith or limited thinking can cause failure! It's always an idea problem!

Those qualities of mind and spirit which enabled Walt Kallestad to achieve his God-given dream are communicated to you in this book. The principles and guidelines for overcoming financial obstacles are here. You will learn how to overcome the real and "perceived as real" roadblocks that you face.

So take a step of faith! Dare to dream a new dream! Let God decide the scope, the breadth, and the depth of your ministry. Learn these dynamic principles that will enable God to crown your efforts with success!

God loves you and so do I.

Robert H. Schuller

INTRODUCTION

by Lyle E. Schaller

The treasurer reports to the September meeting of the governing board that, on the basis of the contributions received for the first eight months of the year, plus projections drawn from the last four months of the previous year, it appears your church will end the year with a substantial deficit.

How will your leaders respond? The most attractive response may be to spend the balance of the evening seeking places where expenditures can be reduced sufficiently to offset that anticipated deficit.

Perhaps someone will propose that instead of cutting expenditures, a special appeal should be made to the members to raise sufficient extra money in contributions to cover that projected deficit.

One difference between these two responses is the first probably will enhance the degree of pessimism and low expectations among the people while the second is more likely to increase optimism, to raise the level of congregational self-esteem and to create the possibility of a congregation-wide celebration.

A second difference is cutbacks tend to be contagious. A cutback in expenditures may encourage those who want to cut back on staff, program, ministry and outreach. By contrast, a challenge to the members for sacrificial giving to offset that deficit is more likely to strengthen the congregation and to encourage others to come forth with new challenges. The Christian faith teaches that God repeatedly challenges us to lift up and utilize the gifts He has given us.

From a long terms perspective, however, both the decision to cut back and the decision to challenge the members for second mile giving are less than perfect responses to that anticipated deficit.

A far better long range approach is to look at the larger picture and to focus on the life, spirit, commitment and climate of the congregation. Preventive maintenance is superior to problem solving.

That is what this book is about. It is both an inspiring case study of the pilgrimage of one pastor and one congregation and a detailed, lucid, practical and Biblically-based prescription on how to strengthen the faith of a congregation so financial crises can be transferred into opportunities for God to bless the lives of both individuals and the entire parish.

This is a story of joy. It is the story of the joy that can be a product of faithful and obedient servanthood to God, it is the story of a congregation called the Community Church of Joy and it is the story of a pastor who has survived tragedies and overcome barriers to experience the joy that is a response to servanthood.

This is a story that must be shared with influential and widely respected leaders in your congregation who take too seriously the warnings of the world about financial caution and tend to be barriers to expanding ministry, rather than channels for God's love and grace.

This is a story that can inspire a new vision among the clergy and within the lay leadership of every congregation that is open to a new approach to church finances. This is a story that can be a handbook for the leaders of every local church where pessimism limits both the vision and the outreach of that community.

This is a story that will bring tears to your eyes, joy to your heart and renewal to your congregation!

LYLE E. SCHALLER
Yokefellow Institute

GETTING A NEW START AND A NEW HEART

"*W*ell, Reverend, what side are you going to be on?" The question was asked by a church member following my very first service in my new congregation. He certainly caught me by surprise. I stumbled for a response. My rather flippant answer was, "Well, I guess I'm going to be on God's side." Then I smiled at him. He grunted something and stomped off, clearly not amused.

Just a few weeks later, one of our prominent leaders tried to punch it out with another member of our church council after a Sunday morning worship service. What had I gotten myself into at this place called Community Church of Joy?

As the days passed, more troublesome signs surfaced. First, an official from the Lutheran Church headquarters called to say that Community Church of Joy had paid nothing on a $272,000 loan made to the church three years earlier. The official also said that a $10,000 mission pledge made by our church was not being fulfilled.

Then someone from the State of Arizona Tax Department called the church to tell us that tax-exempt papers had not been properly filed and that we owed them several thousand dollars in taxes.

Problems continued to emerge and I realized there were enormous "obstacles of opportunity" ahead of us. Having been trained as a theologian, not as a financier, I remember saying repeatedly, "Oh, Lord, what should I do now? Why in the world did you send me to a place with so many financial hurdles?"

Early in my ministry at Community Church of Joy I also learned that there was a great deal of dissension throughout the congregation. There were people who actually said they hated each other!

HELPFUL LESSONS

My father-in-law told me a story shortly before I came to this new congregation. In the church where he worshipped, there had been many heated debates about whether to build on their present location or elsewhere. The conflicts generated by that building issue seemed to bring out the very worst in people.

My father-in-law's position on the building issue was well known in the congregation. On a particular Sunday morning as he walked into church, another parishioner approached him and stuck his tongue out at him. It was the last place on earth my father-in-law thought he'd be "tongued."

Clearly, positive things cannot happen in an atmosphere of conflict. A positive environment needs to be established before finances will flourish. No one gives money nor manages it well when they're mad. So often it seems that when relationships fall apart, so do the finances.

My first lesson about church finances was learned when I was only five years old. My father was an ordained Lutheran pastor whose ministry spanned nearly fifty years. One Sunday morning after the church service, I marched up to him and said, "I want to be a professional usher when I grow up."

"Well, Son, may I ask why you want to be a professional usher?"

"Because when they take up the offering during the church service, they sure get a lot of money!"

Dad straightened me out. He explained that the ushers couldn't keep the money they collected. He said that the money given by people to God every Sunday was used for the work of the church.

"Those offerings are important to keep the church operating smoothly. And besides," Dad continued, smiling, "it really isn't a lot of money." There was more truth to that than I understood then.

It's no secret that adequate finances are important to a successful church, just as they are important to successful people. To make great dreams come true, money is essential. I have watched many churches, religious groups, and great social action programs, as well as businesses and individuals, stop dreaming great dreams, stop praying expectant prayers, and stop planning extraordinary plans because their financial resources slowly dried up or were drastically reduced.

As I considered the obstacles faced by Community Church of Joy, I wondered how we'd overcome them. I asked God yet again why I'd been sent to this place. I reflected on my personal journey to the ordained ministry, filled with obstacles of another kind.

JOURNEY TO THE MINISTRY

As I was growing up, I remember many nights when my father would come home from his ministry in the church nearly broken hearted. Sometimes he'd actually sit down and cry.

Create
A Positive
Climate
Wherever You
Go

There seemed to be so much pain and so many problems in the various churches.

I've always loved, respected, and admired the church. However, in those days, I concluded it would be much less painful to be a lay person. That way I could support the pastors completely, making sure they felt loved and encouraged. It literally took a miracle to lead me to become an ordained pastor.

In 1975, I was Director of Evangelism at Prince of Peace Lutheran Church in Burnsville, Minnesota. I was sent to the Institute on Church Growth at Garden Grove Community Church, California, now known as the Crystal Cathedral. My wife, Mary, and our two small children, Patrick and Shawn, accompanied me on this trip. We stayed with our friends Warren and Louise in the Los Angeles area.

During a Friday morning session of the conference, a man interrupted the speaker and said, "I have an emergency phone call for Walt Kallestad." My heart raced and my hands started to perspire. I was ushered to the nearest telephone in the courtyard.

I heard Louise's voice on the other end of the line saying, "Walt, something terrible has happened. Patrick wandered out by the swimming pool when no one saw him and he fell in. We just found him. He was unconscious and he wasn't breathing. The paramedics are here, and they'll bring him to the hospital by our place." She gave me directions to the hospital.

Tears poured down my cheeks as I placed the receiver back on the phone. I was rushing to the parking lot when Dr. Robert Schuller caught up to me. He asked about my emergency phone call.

When I explained what had happened, Dr. Schuller calmly asked, "Do you believe in miracles?"

"Y...y...yes," I stammered. Oh, I believed they happened in the Bible, but I wasn't as confident about miracles happening in the present time.

Dr. Schuller put his arm firmly around my shoulders. He prayed quickly that a miracle would happen for Patrick in his crisis. I thanked him for his prayer and hurried to my car.

Later, I learned that while I was driving to the hospital, praying all the way, Dr. Schuller had interrupted the conference training session to practice what he has always preached. Under his guidance, 500 pastors and lay leaders from around the world prayed for Patrick with me.

When I arrived at the hospital, I ran into the emergency room where I was met by my wife, Mary. She was sobbing. We held each other and cried together.

Mary explained that while she had been feeding Shawn, our little six-month old daughter, Patrick had wandered outside through the patio door. She had watched him sweeping with a little broom some distance from the pool, and she thought that he would be safe. Looking outside moments later, she was horrified to see the broom floating in the pool. Mary lay Shawn on the floor and rushed outside.

Patrick's lifeless body was floating in the swimming pool. Mary jumped into the cold water with her nightgown on. Pulling Patrick out of the pool, she tried to breathe lifegiving air into his breathless lungs, but nothing happened. She worked on Patrick for what seemed to be hours. He wasn't responding.

Finally, she screamed out, "Help me! Don't let him die! Please, God, help me!" Then she breathed into his tiny lungs again and heard a faint whimper. Louise heard her cries and called for the paramedics. When they arrived soon after, they went efficiently to work, trying to save our son's life.

The paramedics suspected that Patrick's lungs were filled with water. They also indicated that there could be brain damage and other complications. Then they picked him up and started the emergency run to the hospital with sirens blaring.

While Mary was describing the ordeal to me, the emergency room doctor came out. He said that Patrick seemed to be all right. Even now it's nearly impossible to describe the enormous relief and joy we felt at that moment. Mary and I hugged each other, saying, "Thank you, Lord!"

They admitted Patrick to the hospital overnight for observation and further medical care. The next day, an examination of Patrick's x-rays indicated that initially he'd had water in his lungs. But something miraculous had happened. The water had disappeared! Furthermore, there was no brain damage nor any other apparent complications.

The doctor said that we were very lucky parents. I smiled, acknowledging his remarks. But deep in my heart, I knew it was much more than luck. It was the miraculous work of God.

Patrick was released that same morning. The doctor delivered a very stern lecture to us on pool safety. Then he added, "You know, it really is a miracle that he survived." Mary and I understood fully that indeed it was a miracle.

From the hospital, we took Patrick with us back to the Garden Grove Community Church. They were in the midst of a closing Communion service at the conference I had been attending. We all went together to the altar and re-dedicated our family as a whole, as well as our individual lives, to letting the world know how magnificent and wonderful our God is.

It was during this time that I made my final decision to become an ordained minister. I wanted to become as well-tooled and equipped as possible to serve God in as mighty a way as I could.

The skeptics—those who want things to be scientifically provable—challenged my decision by asking, "But what if Patrick had died or had suffered severe brain damage?" My response was that the "what if's" in life are impossible to deal with. I believed with all my heart, then as now, that God would have worked in a dynamic and profound way in my life regardless of the outcome. God's power, love, joy, peace and encouragement are not circumstantial; rather, they are "certain and substantial."

I have learned that "Why?" is the wrong question. "God, why did this have to happen?" That's impossible to answer. It's the "What?" question that's more helpful and purposeful. "God, what can I do now that this event has happened in my life?" And also, "Loving Lord, what do you want to do in and through me?"

My deepest desire since that time has been to spend the rest of my life caring for people and enthusiastically telling the world how wonderful and great God is. I have asked God to take of my time, talents, and finances to help people discover God's love for them. People everywhere need to know what God's promise means:

> *"No eye has seen, no ear has heard, no mind has conceived what God has prepared for those who love him."*
>
> (I Corinthians 2:9 NIV)

My deep love and passion for God's beautiful people were a constant source of encouragement and delight during my seminary training. All during that time, I dreamed of a church filled with perfect people, which was neither fair nor realistic.

One person put it very well when he said, "A church is not a sanctuary for saints; rather, it is a hospital for sinners."

*A Church
Is Not
A Sanctuary
For Saints.
Rather, It Is
A Hospital
For Sinners.*

Certainly, when you gather sinners together in one place, you will have some problems. The key lesson to remember once again is that a positive climate needs to be created in order for great things to transpire.

THE EARLY MONTHS AT CHURCH OF JOY

At Community Church of Joy, the positive and loving climate needed to develop a mission and ministry of excellence seemed far away in my earliest days there. Instead of improving, almost everything got worse. Of the approximately 250 to 300 members present when I arrived, in only six months' time, the congregation had "un-grown" to about 125 members. I was devastated. I quickly calculated that in another six months everyone would be gone and I would simply close up the place and wander the streets looking for a job.

During this time, the meetings with the church's leaders turned into shouting matches. We always found ourselves arguing about *money*! Someone would bring up a great idea and it would be blown off because we couldn't afford it. There were so many creative and innovative things some of us wanted to pursue. We were told *no*. There just wasn't any money.

The fall of 1978 marked my first congregational meeting as the senior pastor of Joy. It was a painful experience. The major topic of discussion was my salary. Before I entered the seminary, I was earning $17,000 annually. After additional years of graduate school, my starting annual salary at Community Church of Joy was $11,000 plus housing and car allowance. With a wife and two children to support, it was financially tight for us.

I learned at that meeting just how emotional money matters can become. The big controversy was whether I should receive a $300 or $500 per year raise. Hearing the arguments and heated debate, you'd have thought a million dollars was the issue.

During that congregational shouting match, my worth and integrity as a person and as a pastor seemed to be on trial. I knew I wasn't perfect, but I hadn't realized how far from perfect! As I listened, I felt the beginning of a fever. I was shaking and my stomach was churning. When the marathon meeting was over, I went home and was sick. I was devastated mentally, emotionally, physically, and spiritually.

THE LAST STRAW

A few days later, the whole Church of Joy situation came to a fiery head. I received a frantic phone call from the director of the preschool which was renting space in the church. She told me that the church kitchen was on fire.

My initial thought was, "Let it burn!" But I told her I'd be right there. She had called the fire department, and they were on their way, too.

As I sat down in my car to drive to my burning church, I began to weep. All of the pressures—finances, people, unresolved conflicts, and shattered dreams—were too much.

I pressed my head against the steering wheel and through my sobbing I cried out, "Please help me, God. I can't do it without you. I surrender my entire life and the life of my church to you. You take charge! If great things happen, I promise that I will give you all the honor and credit. Amen."

When I finished praying, I felt as though a ten-ton weight had been lifted from my shoulders. I could literally feel a new enthusiasm begin to well up within me.

By the time I arrived at the church, the fire in the building was extinguished. But there was a new flame burning inside of me. Nothing had changed, but I was different because God had given me a new attitude. And with my new attitude came a confident and courageous calm. I felt new strength, new energy, new perseverance. This verse from the Bible filled my mind:

"Do you not know? Have you not heard? The Lord is the everlasting God, the Creator of the ends of the earth. He will not grow tired or weary, and his understanding no one can fathom. He gives strength to the weary and increases the power of the weak. Even youths grow tired and weary, and young men stumble and fall; but those who hope in the Lord will renew their

*strength. They will soar on wings like eagles; they will
run and not grow weary; they will walk and not be
faint."*

(Isaiah 40:28-31 NIV)

ENTHUSIASM IS CONTAGIOUS

An interesting transformation occurred when God planted a
new love for the people of Joy in my heart. During the following
days and months, I sensed in myself a new unconditional com-
passion and non-judgmental love for the people of Joy.

Because my attitude was more positive, I became more productive. Times were still tough and many negative people at Joy
were tough, too. Our problems were enormous, but I had surrendered total control to God. It no longer depended upon my limited abilities, but on God's unlimited resources.

*Enthusiasm
Is
Contagious*

Important events often begin with a simple decision. One year into my ministry, and with God's encouragement, I decided to become a warm, friendly person in the form of a warm, friendly hugger. I would stand at the door following the Sunday services and hug people as they left for the day. I wanted people to have the gift of a lift. I believed that smiles and hugs would be a great way to give that gift.

Up to that point, I hadn't always found it easy to hug another person. I was brought up in a strict, reserved Norwegian home. Public displays of affection were not encouraged.

I can still vividly picture my mom and dad, my three sisters, and myself parked downtown in a small Minnesota town on a Friday night. Friday nights were what we called "town nights." People cruised down main street, which was only two or three blocks long, gaping at one another eating popcorn or ice cream, or watching people just strolling along. Whenever a couple would pass our car holding hands or pausing to embrace, my parents made it very clear how disgusting they thought it was.

During my courtship time, I had to work hard to overcome hang-ups I had acquired about holding hands and embracing. My parents, too, have come to understand the importance of a loving hug.

I'll never forget my first attempt at being a hugger at Community Church of Joy. The first person out the door that morning was a big, bearded man who had yelled at me a few days earlier about church finances. When I saw him coming, I mentally reviewed my commitment to hug everybody. There were no exceptions. Everybody meant everybody.

I reached out my arms, closed my eyes, and hugged him, wondering all the while if he'd hit me. That first hug was like embracing a telephone pole. There was absolutely no response. I heard the man grunt and then he was on his way. But the next hug was better, easier, and the next hug easier still.

This enthusiastic spirit was contagious. People in the congregation started inviting their friends to attend church with them. We began to hold our heads higher. We actually talked without yelling about ministry needs involving money. The changes didn't happen overnight, but they were significant.

*A Hug Is
The Gift
Of A Lift!*

Hugging is now part of my life and part of the lives of the people of our congregation. Every Sunday morning, the first thing we do is sing:

"This is the day that the Lord has made; let us rejoice and be glad in it."

(Psalm 118:24 NIV)

Then we turn to each other and say, "God loves you and delights in you." Next, we extend a warm, friendly greeting through a hug or an enthusiastic handshake. Over time, this has helped us to establish a climate of joy, beauty, love, warmth, and inspiration.

Our small band of 250-300 church men, women, and children has grown to more than 3,200 people in eight short years. It's exhilarating that the excitement to support the church financially has grown as well. In 1978, when I arrived at Joy, the giving for the entire year was around $45,000. Now we have a yearly budget of almost $1.5 million. A climate for financial progress has been created.

How did that happen? It was extremely challenging. I will share with you some practical, helpful principles that can be used to help individuals personally and professionally with their finances. These principles evolved out of real life circumstances. They have been tested and found to be extremely successful. I thank God for these great discoveries. Because of them, there is no doubt that *anything* is possible. It's exciting to know that the best is yet to be.

Sometimes, however, before things get better, they get worse. By 1984, things were beginning to look better for Community Church of Joy. Then, suddenly it appeared that the bottom was about to fall out of everything.

On a clear, beautiful Sunday morning, I stood before the congregation to tell them that within seven days, we were facing the possibility of being locked up as a church and shut down as a ministry.

"This Is
The Day
That The
Lord Has
Made;
Let Us
Rejoice
And Be Glad
In It."

(Psalm 118:23)

A FINANCIAL CRISIS

*T*his particular financial crisis hadn't developed overnight. It had taken years to bring the church to the point of being permanently locked up.

My passion to help people solve problems, heal hurts and fill needs had been the driving force behind my commitment to full-time ministry. I had been confident that if I took care of the "ministry," the money would take care of itself. That was not responsible management. Anyone serious about being an effective Christian needs to pay careful attention to both areas.

It will be helpful to look at the stages of growth that led to Community Church of Joy's being threatened with lockout by the bank.

GOOD STAFFING IS AN ASSET

Some time ago, I asked John Vucurevich, a prominent businessman of great integrity, if he had any special words of wisdom for businesses and organizations. He pondered a moment and then he said, "If I could share one thing that would help make companies, corporations and churches successful, it would be to always invest in people, not in buildings and programs. People should always be considered first."

I have observed during visits to over 1,000 different churches, colleges and other private institutions that you need staff to grow. When you are short-staffed, you either become maintenance-minded or you begin to decline. People are the greatest resource in the world.

Staffing that is done right is a good investment. You can consider it an asset. Uncommitted, unmotivated staff can become a serious liability, ultimately costing much more than their salary. At the end of this chapter, you will find a list of nine key questions to assist you in hiring good staff.

I believe that dynamic, committed, loyal staff pay for themselves. Through their work and ministry, such a staff can be so inspiring that people will support them, both personally and financially.

As the needs of Joy were growing, it became evident that we would require more staff to help. And so I added staff as fast as I possibly could.

GIVE AND TAKE

As I added people to our staff, growth in membership increased. Our growing staff became very productive. Soon they were requesting program money. It's pointless to hire good employees if you can't give them the tools and resources to do their jobs.

The costs of our programs began to grow rapidly. This didn't set off any warning signals, because everything seemed to be working the way it was supposed to. Money was tight, but I was sure that everyone would respond to the great things that were happening by financially supporting them.

That did happen to some degree. But even though many people were being served, too many of them weren't supporting the church financially.

Historically, the church has always had passive members who take the services and programs offered by the church for granted. They expect the church to exhibit a spirit of giving, but it does not occur to them to give generously to the church.

The sad reality is that even the affluent sometimes become passive members of the church, perhaps without being aware of it. They have the resources, but are not always willing to give generously and sacrificially. It can be a brand new day in the church and the world when that changes. However, as things stand now, there is often an inequity in a church's giving.

THE 20/80 RULE

The 20/80 Rule states that 20% of the people will provide 80% of the support to an organization. For example, if the need is $100,000 and 100 people are involved, 20 people will give $80,000 and the remaining 80 people will give only $20,000. Business leaders say that this is true in the job force as well. 20% of the people provide 80% of the productivity.

*People
Are
The Greatest
Resource
In
The World*

At Community Church of Joy, the same 20% are continually challenged to become even more generous and sacrificial, and they respond positively. The great irony which sometimes perpetuates this inequity in giving is that it's usually more productive to work with someone already committed to giving generously than it is to spend time with someone who has not yet decided to be a giving person.

TIME TO BUILD...BUT HOW?

Community Church of Joy grew rapidly. The 200 doubled. The 400 grew to 800. Soon the 800 increased to 1600, and then to 3200.

One Sunday morning in 1981, our rather small building, designed for 350 people, was so overcrowded that worshippers had to stand. One woman fainted from the heat. We obviously had a serious problem with lack of space. Something had to be done. It was time to build a bigger building.

We spent a lot of time examining our needs. Then we began work on designing a new building to meet the pressing need we had for more space. The congregation voted unanimously to construct a new $750,000 sanctuary.

There was excitement and expectation as the building project took shape. Although we certainly needed the space, because of personnel and programs, our cash flow was tight. The big, unanswered question was, "How will we pay for this new building?"

We decided to undertake a building fund drive. We discussed different ways of doing the best possible job in raising the $750,000. Some said that members and friends of Joy were already giving all they could. How could anyone expect them to give any more money?

Reflecting on that statement, I knew that people always give what they want to give. If someone decides to give more, they will give more.

Inspiring ideas generate inspired giving. Enthusiastic people who are excited about their ideas attract generous giving. Outstanding projects create a desire to sacrificially support them. Most of the people I know want to be part of something great. They want to associate with winning opportunities.

*Inspiring Ideas
Generate
Inspired Giving*

After much discussion, the church leadership hired a fundraising consultant. This consultant helped us to get organized and to develop an accountability system. We knew we needed many volunteer workers to accomplish the task.

Everything went extremely well. The stewardship drive raised approximately $600,000 over a three-year period. Our initial goal had been reached. The leadership joined me in believing that the hundreds of new members joining the church would give the remaining $150,000 we needed.

We started to build. Constructing a new building is an energizing event. I could hardly wait to get to work each day to see what was happening. It was much like the joy you experience when you're building your own dream house, only this was God's house.

The enthusiasm was contagious. Worship attendance picked up. People were anxious to see what had been completed the previous week. The offerings were higher because people wanted to be part of this significant project. Everyone's spirits were soaring.

A crucial building decision had to be made. It was evident that the church was growing and would continue to grow very fast. A major concern was that the new building might not be big enough. We were designing a structure with 750 seats inside and 750 seats outside. By doubling the size, it would be possible to accommodate 3,000 people. After a great deal of prayer, many midnight discussions and much deliberation, the decision was made to "go for it." Certainly our growth would finance the added cost...wouldn't it?

PLUNGING AHEAD WITH ABANDON

We plunged ahead. The cost rose quickly from $750,000 to $1.2 million. Part of the $1.2 million was the cost of furnishings, pews, carpet, sound system, organ and numerous other items. I now believe that furnishings shouldn't be ordered until they're paid for. Furnishings for a new building usually can be obtained through special gifts and memorials.

When we discovered that we'd need considerably more

money, I went to see a friend who was president of a local bank. I shared with him our exciting project and asked for a loan of $500,000. The banker agreed to give the church the loan.

From the beginning of the church, all of its land and building financing was borrowed money. The first $272,000 our church needed was borrowed by selling bonds to our members. The next $750,000 was borrowed from a bonding company that sold bonds all over the country. Then we borrowed the additional $500,000 that I'd negotiated. The total debt load of nearly $1.5 million was extremely heavy.

Because of all the debt, too much of our ministry money was being used up in mortgage payments. This heavy burden grew heavier with each passing day. The cash flow dried up. All of our resources and energies became focused on our debts and not on our dreams. This bondage negatively impacted the staff, the leaders, and the congregation members and friends of Community Church of Joy. Positive attitudes deteriorated rapidly.

URGENT NEED FOR REFINANCING

We started to fall behind in setting aside money for a large mortgage payment coming due in six months. But we weren't worried since we'd decided to refinance all of our debts and place them on a 30-year mortgage plan instead of the short term mortgage plan we'd been on to that point. Most people have 30-year home mortgages, and that's what we were trying to get.

As time passed, it appeared less and less likely that anyone would be willing to refinance our entire debt for 30 years. However, there was a bonding company that agreed to consider refinancing a portion of the debt. They talked about taking the $500,000 on which we had a one-year agreement and extending it to at least 15 years.

An extraordinary amount of my time and the time of other leaders was getting tied up in the management of our debt. I started despising debt. I saw it as an enemy. Debt had virtually made the church a slave to the lenders.

THE BAD NEWS ARRIVES

We were only seven days from completion of all of the refinancing and from a $78,000 payment that was to be included in the refinancing.

That's when we received the dreadful news that we needed $60,000 cash up front for the closing costs before the bonding company would continue with the refinancing. Further, they'd decided not to include the $78,000 payment in the refinancing package. They demanded immediate payment of the $78,000, concluding by saying, "Be assured that if you do not pay us the $78,000 in seven days, we have the right to send our men out to your church to padlock all the doors and throw you off the property."

Everything I'd prayed about, worked on, cried over, hoped for and dreamed of was about to be taken away. But even greater than my personal concerns was my concern for all the members, staff, friends and acquaintances of Community Church of Joy. How could they be asked to accept a total lockup of the church?

WAS IT ALL OVER?

For nearly eight years I had watched spiritual, emotional, and numerical growth take place at Church of Joy. In one week's time, it could all be over. I felt like a failure. What was I going to do? How was I going to break the news to the people of Joy?

Shortly before it was time to tell the congregation, I went for a ride with the congregation president. He was in high level management with AT&T and I was confident he'd have some guidance. But when I told him what happened, he broke down and cried with me.

I learned more about the hard, cold facts of finances in that crisis-filled week than I had learned in all my 37 years. I promised God that if I ever got out of that terrible mess, I would never let the church borrow another penny.

A MIRACLE IN THE MAKING

We made a decision to present the news to the leaders and to as many other people as possible on the following Wednesday. Then on Sunday, we would go to our people and tell them the truth. Those who came to church that day would determine the destiny of the ministry.

All week, there was calm certainty in my heart about what was going to happen. But in my head, in my stomach and in the rest of me there was tension and an unbearable ache.

On the one hand, it was exciting to see what God was about to do, but on the other, it was difficult to face up to the financial mess that had been created. I felt that God was close. I knew God would love me whatever happened, but I felt that at any moment the lions might be released into our special arena.

Our Wednesday meeting with the leaders was packed with emotion. The congregation president explained in detail what had happened. Then he said, "We need $78,000 this week or our ministry is over." I heard gasps, sobs, sighs.

One person said, "Well, let's borrow the money." Mercifully, everyone laughed and passed over that suggestion.

Then someone else said, "Well, we'll just have to get the $78,000 we need. There's no other option." I prayed that everyone would feel that way. I longed for the people of Joy to believe that God could make it possible.

After an emotionally charged week and a long restless Saturday night, the dreaded Sunday morning dawned. I began that day as I had each Sunday for the past eight years by saying,

> *"This is the day that the Lord has made. Let us rejoice and be glad in it."*
>
> (Psalm 118:24 NIV)

Those words open every gathering at Joy—even funerals. Joy and rejoicing do not depend upon circumstances, but rather upon the certainty of Jesus Christ. Whatever is happening to me, I can experience joy. Whatever crisis I may be facing I can rejoice. The Bible tells us:

> *"Rejoice in the Lord always. I will say it again: Rejoice!"*
>
> (Philippians 4:4 NIV)

I knew there were visitors with us that morning. I knew there were some people present who'd stayed away from church for years, because every time they came all they heard was talk about money. There were people attending the worship service with broken hearts and bruised spirits who needed to hear a message of hope. How would all these people respond? Oh, how I prayed that everyone would understand!

We continued the service by singing hymns of joy, celebration and expectation. We read a Bible story together. We prayed together. Then I presented the president of the congregation to the people attending the worship service.

He told the whole story and concluded his remarks by saying, "Your response today will determine whether we will worship here again next Sunday." Then he cried. Regaining his composure, he asked the congregation to pray with him. Finally, he invited the people of Joy to come and lay their gifts at the altar.

I was seated in the front row with the congregation. I had been praying fervently throughout the morning. When the congregation president sat down, I glanced at people, trying to read their expressions.

At first there was stillness and silence. I held my breath, waiting. Gradually, I heard sounds of purses opening, billfolds coming out of pockets, check blanks being torn out of checkbooks and other papers rustling. I sensed that something incredible was happening.

*Joy
Is Not
Circumstantial...
Joy Is The
Certainty
Of Jesus Christ*

There were three services that Sunday morning. At the last of them, when the invitation was made to come forward to lay special gifts on the altar, a young boy marched up to the front of the church carrying his Snoopy bank. He had saved his pennies, nickels, dimes and quarters all his life. He literally was giving everything he had to Jesus that morning. When I saw his sacrificial gift, tears streamed down my cheeks.

Other people came to the altar with money they, too, had been saving for years—some for down payments on new homes—and they gave it all to God. Even some who were unemployed shared generously. One of those persons was the head of the maintenance department of Joy who'd been released because of this crisis.

Later that afternoon when the flow of people with checks and cash had subsided, we'd received far more than the $78,000 that was needed. The miracle of God came to $150,000!

*Give God
A Standing
Ovation
Today*

When the good news was announced the following Sunday, there was a "celebration of celebrations." Through all our troubled times, God had given us tougher faith and more tender hearts. We all gave God a standing ovation. Our hearts leaped for joy. The victory had been won. The future once again was filled with fantastic opportunities.

The first major hurdle—that of the $78,000—had been overcome. Now we had to deal with the cause of the crisis. We needed to ensure that nothing like this would happen ever again.

*Tough Times
Produce
Tough Faith
And
Tender Hearts*

NINE KEY HIRING QUESTIONS

Some good questions to ask a prospective staff person during the interview are:

1. What are your greatest strengths?
2. What are your greatest weaknesses?
   (How does this person perceive himself or herself?)
3. Why do you want to have this job?
   (What is this person's real motivation?)
4. What do you see yourself doing five years, ten years, or twenty years from now?
   (Where is this person going?)
5. What do you most enjoy doing?
6. What do you least enjoy doing?
   (What will this person spend most of his/her time doing?)
7. How long do you see yourself doing this particular job?
   (How committed is this person?)
8. What do you understand to be the vision for this mission?
   (Where does this person see the whole organization going and what is seen as most important?)
9. Describe for me your ultimate dream job.
   (What does this person really want to do with his/her life?)

Certainly there are more questions to ask, but I have found these nine to be very helpful in the initial screening process.

MONEY MANAGEMENT

$\mathcal{F}$ollowing our $150,000 miracle, the financial institutions, members of the congregation, and numerous people throughout the community were simply amazed. Clearly something extraordinary had happened. Many people said they had never seen anything like it. No one could have anticipated that soon another miracle would be required.

STRUCTURING FOR SUCCESS

The $150,000 gave us enough to meet the $78,000 mortgage payment. What was left over paid off all the 30-60-90-day bills we had accumulated over the previous twelve months. It was wonderful to have a fresh start.

The time had come to structure the finances of the church in such a way that future crises could be avoided. Because of our miracle, the people who held our mortgages all agreed to keep our loans the way they were for one more year.

We had just 365 days to establish our credibility as money managers so we could then persuade someone to refinance us. Refinancing would improve our cash flow, thereby enabling our ministry to move forward.

We took stock of every cent we had in hand. We calculated all funds we anticipated receiving for the rest of the year. Then we looked at our daily, weekly, monthly and yearly commitments. It didn't take long to confirm that our outgo was exceeding our income.

Our typical weekly offerings amounted to about $10,000. Actual weekly expenses, including benevolences, mortgage payments, fixed expenses, salaries and various program needs, totaled $15,000.

It doesn't take a financier to figure out that if you're going in the hole at the rate of $5,000 per week, in just ten weeks you'll be $50,000 in debt. While I believe in faith and in the essence of faith which is risk, I also believe that it wouldn't have been fair to impose our "faith" on unsuspecting creditors.

Our witness to vendors, to banks, and to others in the community needed to be positive. By making creditors wait for their payment, we were essentially asking them to help finance our ministry.

CHRISTIAN CREDIBILITY

I believe Christians should have a highly credible financial record. We should be known for paying our bills promptly. Nevertheless, I have discovered that many companies and financial institutions refuse to do business with Christians and churches because many don't pay their bills on time. When that happens, word gets out not to do business with Christians because they will take advantage of you. My prayer is for this negative witness to change.

In light of those considerations, I deeply desired that our church might establish its financial credibility. In order to accomplish that, we had to take some drastic steps to match our income to our $15,000 outgo. It was time to cut expenses.

CUTBACKS CAN CREATE COMEBACKS

Sometimes cutbacks are essential for comebacks. I have a tree in my backyard that needs to be cut back to the base every year in order for it to flourish in the spring and summer months. Still, it's one thing to know you need to cut back, and quite another to actually do it.

Where were we going to cut? Everything we had going for us in ministry was needed. I'd have loved cutting out our mortgage payment. I dreamed about using that $5,000 each week for mission and ministry instead.

The weight of our debt was a dreadful burden. I vowed I'd do everything possible for us to become "debt free." Never again would I borrow even one penny. I believe that is the best financial decision I have ever made.

As I reviewed the cash flow statement, I determined that our 10% benevolence commitment was a must. I couldn't ask our people to tithe 10% of their income, according to Biblical principles, if our church was not a model in that regard. That 10% should be part of the budget for any successful church, corporation, or individual. Look at what God promised to those who tithe:

> *"Bring the whole tithe into the storehouse, that there may be food in my house. 'Test Me in this,' says the Lord God Almighty, 'and see if I will not throw open the floodgates of heaven and pour out so much blessing that you will not have room enough for it.'"*
>
> (Malachi 3:10 NIV)

Cutbacks
Can Create
Comebacks

I have discovered that tithers are often the best money managers. When you honor and put God first in your finances, you will be given wisdom to better manage the other 90%. Over the years, we have seen some fantastic things happen to people who have made a commitment to tithe.

The next cash flow item at Joy was fixed expenses. The weekly costs for electricity, water, office supplies, toilet paper, postage, cleaning supplies and other things seemed reasonable for an organization as large as ours. Still, these costs had to be cut.

By reducing mailings (an important avenue of communication), cutting electrical costs and water usage, encouraging people to bring a roll of toilet paper and designated cleaning supplies, and by making other cuts, we managed to trim our $1,500 weekly fixed assets to a bare bones $1,000 per week.

The hardest area involved cutting back the staff. People caring for people is what made our ministry great. Every staff person was an essential, significant part of our team. They were not only working partners, they were friends.

I couldn't face this alone. Our congregation president, the director of our personnel committee, my closest associate, and I sat down one afternoon to make some of the most difficult decisions of our lives.

After hours of deliberation, prayer and hard work, we concluded that the staffing budget had to be cut by $1,500 per week. That meant that ten positions would be eliminated and all the remaining personnel would be required to take a 25% reduction in pay.

I couldn't believe this was happening. I asked God repeatedly why this had to be, realizing all the while that I would never know. The better question was, "What?" What was I going to do now that all of these things had happened?

*"For Nothing
Is
Impossible
With God"*

(LUKE 1:37)

A TIME TO GROW

Was I going to quit? No. I'm not a quitter. Would I become negative? No. Remaining grateful in the midst of a negative experience is the only way to survive as well as to thrive. I wanted not only to *go through* all this, I wanted to *grow through* it all. I was determined not to be bitter but to become better.

My stomach had been so knotted up and I was so emotionally drained that I hadn't slept well nor had I eaten properly for some time, but I was exercising regularly. I had my quiet time with the Lord every morning, reading three to four chapters from the Bible and spending 30-45 minutes in prayer.

Many positive promises of God flowed through my mind. One day in the book of Joshua, the first chapter, verse nine, I read these words:

> *"Be strong and courageous. Do not be terrified; do not be discouraged, for the Lord your God will be with you wherever you go."*

That is more than "good news." Other verses from the Bible ran through my mind.

> *"For nothing is impossible with God."*
>
> (Luke 1:37 NIV)

Phillipians 4:13 was my theme verse throughout my college years. I had these words printed in bold letters and taped up on my desk:

> *"I can do everything through Him who gives me strength."*

A DAY OF HEARTBREAK

The day arrived to break the news to the staff. Lee Wheeler, president of the congregation, and Rick Johnson, our vice-president in charge of personnel, explained to them in detail everything that was happening financially with our ministry.

Lee wrote the facts and figures on the chalkboard. He explained through his tears that there was a need to eliminate ten full-time and part-time staff people from the payroll and that the remaining personnel would be given a drastic 25% cut in pay. We all wept with him.

With tears streaming down our cheeks, we got down on our knees to pray. My heart literally ached. Through the corridor of our tears, I felt God coming to touch us with love and healing.

I was reminded of the story of Jesus in the Garden of Gethsemane the night before His death. Jesus said,

> *"My soul is overwhelmed with sorrow to the point of death."*
>
> (Mark 14:34 NIV)

Now that's an indescribable heartache. When Jesus' heart felt like breaking and when He was so distraught that He actually sweat drops of blood, He prayed to the loving God He knew He could count on.

In my life I have discovered there is nothing that can happen to me that can destroy me. God is bigger than any problem. God has never let me down. Because of God, even death cannot destroy me. I am continually encouraged by this promise:

> *"Who shall separate us from the love of Christ? Shall trouble or hardship or persecution or famine or nakedness or danger or sword? No. In all these things, we are more than conquerors through Him who loved us. For I am convinced that neither death nor life, neither angels nor demons, neither the present nor the future, nor any powers, neither height nor depth, nor anything else in all creation, will be able to separate us from the love of God that is in Christ Jesus our Lord."*
>
> (Romans 8:35, 37-39 NIV)

Christians are not promised a life free of problems. But they are promised the power to face and deal with their problems.

I like what Dr. Robert Schuller tells us: "Christ can turn problems into possibilities." That's true. Problems produce people with passion. The people who are the most loving, caring, compassionate and encouraging are those who have had enormous problems to overcome in their lives.

God
Is Bigger
Than Any
Problem

Someone expressed it beautifully: "In love's service, only broken hearts will do."

Following that painful staff meeting, I went to my office to prepare myself for calling in each staff member to tell them either that they were no longer on the payroll or that they would receive an immediate 25% pay cut. As I sat in my chair, I told God that a large gift appearing among us would prevent having to go through this horrible experience. I believe God could have bailed us out. God owns it all. Surely one or two million dollars wouldn't have been missed.

However, had God intervened, we would not have grown, stretched, learned and become more God-dependent. Sometimes, we want God to be like Santa Claus. We expect God to be at our beck and call to give us everything we want at the snap of our fingers.

Tough times produce perseverance, character and hope. The Bible tells us that:

*"We also rejoice in our sufferings, because we know
that suffering produces perseverance; perseverance,
character; and character, hope."*

(Romans 5: 3-4 NIV)

After meeting with my staff, my concern was to help those beloved people with the difficult burden being placed on them. Wherever possible, we helped those who were let go to find employment.

These were tough times for each staff member, but they all responded like champions. Those remaining on staff were positive and willing to work even harder. When you hire and surround yourself with great people, you are able to survive absolutely anything.

Within days, rumors were rampant throughout the community. In stores people would stop me to ask if Community Church of Joy was closing up. I even received phone calls from other parts of the country asking me whether we were losing the church.

Everything had gone so well up until that time. We had grown by 1,000% in six and a half years. Our budget had increased over 2,000%. We had a beautiful new sanctuary. Now we were being gossiped about all over the country. I get calls even today from people who are surprised our church is still operating. All in all, it was a very humbling time for me. But God promises to empower the humble.

*In Love's
Service
Only
Broken Hearts
Will Do*

TRAIN YOUR MIND

It's very important to rise above negative, destructive criticism. The more you dwell on what other people are thinking about you, the more paranoid you become. Champions continually train their minds to think about, expect and seek after the best. The Bible tells us how to train our minds:

> *"...whatever is right, whatever is pure, whatever is lovely, whatever is admirable— if anything is excellent or praiseworthy— think about such things."*
> (Philippians 4:8 NIV)

This is the formula for excelling in any area of life.

MOVING ON

Finally, after trimming the staff line item, I looked at the program budget. Even after cutting everything possible in the first four categories without severing the very nerve center of the ministry, we were still committed to spending $10,500 every week—$500 over our goal of $10,000.

That meant that the program budget had to be eliminated completely. When the program people needed some money, they would simply have to be creative in raising it.

CREDIBILITY PAYS OFF

When our expenses exceed our income, we must prune or cut back our expenses. It's tough and sometimes even painful. However, what's the alternative? To fail financially? To ruin our testimony of trust? To have a poor credit rating? To put pressure on our loved ones?

The leaders felt that even though we were short $500 per week, we would work hard to raise that amount. It's interesting to note that this amount and more was raised when our people learned that we had our finances under control.

Attitude is important in financial management. A positive attitude that includes accountability and responsibility is very rewarding. When we were no longer willing to operate by the "seat of our pants" system, we began to see some tremendous results. Staff and leadership credibility grew as people saw our willingness to face the problem. It was amazing how giving increased and special gifts started to come in. I believe that God honored and delighted in the commitment, sacrifice and dedication demonstrated throughout this period of Joy's life.

Champions Train Their Minds To Think About, To Expect, And To Seek After The Best

UNDER NEW MANAGEMENT

Community Church of Joy's creditors, the banks and other mortgage holders received our new management plan and our reporting system, which was very simple.

Weekly income was printed at the top. Weekly expenses were recorded in the simple five-step structure found as a supplement at the end of this chapter. The balance in every checking and savings account was listed. Every penny was accounted for. All expenditures required prior approval.

This kind of discipline is essential, not only to those in the midst of financial difficulty. but even to those who are prospering financially. We are expected to manage our money in a way that will most honor God and be most rewarding to God's people.

My counsel is this: "Without a budget you blow it...with a budget you build it."

The payoff finally came. In February of 1986, Lutheran Brotherhood, a financial institution I'd approached on four previous occasions asking for refinancing, finally agreed to work with us.

"NO" DOESN'T MEAN "NO" FOREVER

It is evident to me that just because someone has said no, it doesn't necessarily mean no forever. If you have been turned down once, the next time you may be "turned on." Never quit! Never give up! Never say never!

I loved it when Dr. Schuller said: "Great people are ordinary people with an extraordinary amount of determination."

It's important to note here that most members, friends and prospective new members who were there when the church went through its crisis did not desert Joy. Some did leave, saying they didn't want to be part of a sinking ship. But the majority stayed and supported each other.

Without A Budget You Blow It...
With A Budget You Build It

In fact, our membership classes were larger than ever. We took in almost 600 new members during our toughest times. Only God could pull off something like that! Certainly we had our share of complaining and negative conversation. But the spirit of Joy grew in strength. As the Bible says:

"Do not grieve, for the joy of the Lord is your strength."
(Nehemiah 8:10 NIV)

Lutheran Brotherhood requested that we submit all of our financial information for their review board. We were informed from the beginning that the refinancing was by no means a sure thing. Never in their history had they loaned even a million dollars to a church, and we were asking for 1.2 million dollars.

After a few weeks of investigation, Lutheran Brotherhood told us that the only way we could possibly qualify was to have the American Lutheran Church, our national headquarters, co-sign the loan. When I heard that I had to go to the ALC, I thought of Lee Iacocca going to the United States Government, trying to convince them to sign off on a loan for the Chrysler Corporation. Well, he did it! I believed it could be done for Community Church of Joy as well.

I met with the ALC officials. They probed through our past and current financial records. They were aware of the financial crisis we had struggled through. They were also aware of our exciting growth and the magnificent $150,000 miracle. Finally, because of the committed, sacrificial people who are a part of Community Church of Joy, they agreed to endorse the loan.

VICTORY DAY
It took several weeks to negotiate all the details with Lutheran Brotherhood. However, everything was finally worked out and we got the financing package that gave our ministry a new beginning. When I received word of their final decision, I wanted to do a victory dance like football players do in the end zone following a touchdown.

Our monthly mortgage payments were cut almost in half.

This freed up mortgage money to use for ministry. What a sweet day! The hard work and dedication had paid off.

Because of a generous anonymous gift, the original 25% pay cut had been reduced to 12%. One of the first things the church leadership wanted to do was to reinstate full salaries for the staff.

*Never
Quit!!!*

It was fun to start dreaming exciting dreams again. The oppression seemed to be delightfully lifted. When new and creative ideas were presented, they were received with greater enthusiasm. We began to look again at new ministry projects. We weren't about to move recklessly ahead, but we were ready to go.

I remembered some unexpected advice I received when Mary and I once visited Boston. We were looking one evening for a nice place to have dinner. In asking around, we were told about Anthony's Pier Four Restaurant, described to us as a world-famous place to eat.

As we entered the restaurant, I saw a picture on the wall of the owner, Mr. Anthony. Alongside the picture stood Mr. Anthony himself. I introduced myself to him. During our brief conversation, I asked, "What is the secret of your great success?"

With a big smile and a sparkle in his eye, Mr. Anthony said, "Well, many people say that I was just lucky. But I have discovered that the harder I work, the luckier I get."

I believe that is true of anything we undertake in our lives. The Bible emphasizes in Proverbs, the tenth chapter, verse four, that:

*"Lazy hands make a man poor, but diligent hands
bring wealth."*

Hard work doesn't burn us out. It's circumstantial pressure that drains us.

Financial struggles are not unique to professional financial management. They are also a part of our personal finances as well. As I confronted the challenges of the church's finances, I also had to confront some personal financial challenges. I came to the point of embarrassment and humiliation before I made the decision to do something about my personal finances. Let's look at what happened.

The Harder You Work The Luckier You Get

SUPPLEMENT TO CHAPTER 3

BUILD YOUR OWN BUDGET

This basic outline for budgeting is useful for most people. It works! (Use illustrations and charts, i.e. 12,000/year, 25,000/year, 50,000/year):

1. Tithe: Honor God with the first 10%
2. Mortgage Payments: house/building payment
3. Fixed Expenses: water, electricity, cleaning supplies, food, savings, insurances, gas, etc.
4. Personal Needs: allowances, doctors, personal improvement
5. Programmatic Needs: programs for business or recreational needs for private needs (such as "spending money")

	$12,000 Month/Year		$25,000 Month/Year		$50,000 Month/Year	
TITHE	100	1000	208	2500	417	5000
MORTGAGE*						
FIXED						
EXPENSE*						
Savings						
Water						
Electricity						
Food						
Insurance						
Car						
PERSONAL NEEDS*						
Medical						
Clothing						
RECREATIONAL*						
Spending Money						
TOTAL		12,000		25,000		50,000

*Fill in amounts

Outgo Must Never Exceed Income

PERSONAL FINANCIAL DISCOVERIES

FINANCIAL EMBARRASSMENT

In addition to all our problems at the church, my personal finances were an embarrassment to me. I needed to apply for a $650 loan to buy an evaporative cooler for my home to help save money on electrical costs.

A woman at the bank took down all the information she needed and went to discuss my request with her supervisor. When she returned, she said, "Sir, your request has been denied. When you start taking responsibility for your finances and when you stop overdrawing your account, you can come back and maybe we will help you."

I was steamed. I stomped out of that bank, mumbling under my breath, "I'll get even with her. That little whippersnapper, who does she think she is? She's so young and immature. Doesn't she know who I am? Why, I have a college degree and four years of graduate school. I deserve more respect than she gave me." I grumbled and complained for many hours after that stinging rejection. I decided I'd do business with another bank.

I considered myself to be an honest, upright citizen. I had never cheated anyone. I had never defaulted on a loan. It was true that I'd been overdrawn three times that year, but only because I forgot to deposit my checks when I should have. I knew I was a man with integrity and credibility, but I was pretty sloppy in managing my finances.

Sometimes we get upset with people when they criticize us because deep in our hearts, we know they're telling us the truth. But our pride makes us defensive and we react in anger.

I had a choice. I could take the woman's advice to become a better money manager or I could be bitter. I opted to get better. It wasn't a matter of earning more money to get into a better financial position. It was a matter of better managing the money I did have.

Success Is Taking Time To Build A Budget And To Stick With It

The budget structure Mary and I built for ourselves eight years ago looks much the same today. Basically only the dollar amounts are different. Thankfully, we earn more money now.

Income	**Expenses**
Salary	God — 10% or more
	Savings
	Mortgage
Other Income	Utilities
	Social Security
	Taxes
	Automobile Loan
	Food
	Clothing
	Recreation
	Insurances
TOTAL _____	TOTAL _____

If the income column does not match or exceed the expenses column, obviously some changes need to be made. To continually spend more than you have coming in could be described as being dishonest. It's promising to pay for a purchase without knowing how you'll do it.

THE CREDIT CARD CON

Credit cards make it easy to spend far beyond one's earnings. Advertisers make seductive appeals to us to buy now and worry later about how we'll pay for it. They're actually encouraging irresponsible money management.

There have been times in my life when I have overextended myself financially with a credit card. My charges far exceeded what I could possibly pay off. So, I ended up paying 21% interest on things I'd bought. By the time I paid off the balance, my purchases cost me two or three times the original price.

One afternoon, I drove to my mother's home and handed her all my credit cards. I confessed to her that I was abusing them and I asked her to keep them until I learned how to be more responsible.

Every year, I receive mail offers of thousands of dollars of credit. If I had accepted all the credit I've been offered, I'd be in prison, because there's no way I could ever have paid it all back with interest!

*Wants Will
Always Exceed
Needs
But Needs Are
Filled With
Prosperous
Seeds*

WANTS WILL ALWAYS EXCEED NEEDS

Wants always exceed needs. Everyone wants nice things. We all want more than we have. But when a person's life becomes controlled and directed by wants, they can easily fail financially. Wants dictate that enough is never enough. Contentment becomes elusive to a want-driven person. Christians handle this struggle by surrendering their wants to the Lord. God promises:

> "And my God will meet all your needs according to His glorious riches in Christ Jesus."
>
> (Philippians 4:19 NIV)

Christ gives us perspective on our wants. He helps us distinguish between a want and a need. Then He promises satisfaction as all of the "real priorities," which are our needs, are met.

WE CAN'T OUTGIVE GOD

We just cannot outgive God. We have been told:

> "It is more blessed (or happy) to give than to receive."
>
> (Acts 20:35 NIV)

Another way God prepares us for being showered with good gifts is shared in the words of Luke:

> "Give, and it will be given to you. A good measure, pressed down, shaken together and running over, will be poured into your lap."
>
> (Luke 6:38a NIV)

I had an experience with God's generosity just before my college years. I was wondering how I could ever pay for my college education. The thousands of dollars needed for tuition, books, room and board, seemed insurmountable. I told God I needed help.

Then I was offered both a high paying construction job and work in a Christian organization that could only pay minimal wages. I felt that God wanted me to work with the Christian organization, which turned out to be the highest paying position of all!

Just weeks before I was to begin my studies, I received a phone call from a farming couple who had known my parents when my dad pastored a church in Elk Point, South Dakota. They called to ask if they could "adopt" me. This special couple didn't have children of their own, and they'd decided to pay my way through college. When I heard this, my heart exploded with joy! God had showered me with a blessing far beyond what I could ever have dreamed or imagined possible. We can't outgive God.

You Can't Outgive God!!!

Another of the many times in my life that I experienced the impossibility of outgiving God was during my seminary internship. I received word that my internship assignment was to be at Northwest Texas Hospital in Amarillo, Texas. My family and I were to move there for nine months. We'd need to rent an apartment and be responsible for our own automobile expenses, food, clothing, insurances, utilities, and all other personal expenses.

I had just made a monthly commitment of $110 to support a particular ministry. I learned I would be earning only $500 per month. How was I going to support my family on the remaining $390? I prayed daily for wisdom, help, and guidance.

Late one night, the telephone rang. It was a friend with whom I hadn't visited for a long time. He said, "I hear you're going to Texas to do your seminary internship. My wife and I have been thinking about you and praying for you and we were encouraged to call to let you know we want to pay for your apartment while you're in Texas."

Deeply grateful, I accepted his generous offer. When I hung up the phone, I screamed, "Fantastic!" I'm sure I woke everyone in our apartment complex. I excitedly told Mary what happened. We truly cannot outgive God!

Certainly, God is the greatest giver of all. A favorite Bible verse expresses the giving nature of our loving Lord:

"For God so loved the world that He gave His one and only Son, that whosoever believes in Him shall not perish but have eternal life."

(John 3:16 NIV)

Amazing! What a God! All of us have so much to learn about giving.

SIGNIFICANT SACRIFICE

A gigantic lesson on giving came during my third year as the pastor of Community Church of Joy. I was pretty satisfied with my 12% giving. I dreamed about the day when I would be able to give away half my income. However, at that particular time in my life with young children, a high mortgage, car expenses, and other financial demands, I was content.

The church had been growing rapidly and it was obvious that we needed a new sanctuary. Growth is exciting, especially when you consider the alternative. Our growth potential was unlimited. The leaders of our church saw the needs and decided to hire a consultant to help us properly manage our growth and our new building program.

One of the first comments this consultant made to me was, "Pastor, this new building program is going to require a great deal of sacrifice. I will be asking not for equal gifts, but rather for equal sacrifice."

He went on to say, "As you consider your sacrifice, you will never be able to ask your people to do anything you are not willing to do yourself." This seemed like good counsel, but I didn't yet know what it would mean to me personally.

As the program unfolded, it came time to make the financial commitments. Mary and I examined our giving. We concluded that we were already giving very generously and sacrificially. After all, we were making the third largest contribution in our congregation and I knew I wasn't earning the third highest salary! We decided we were being sacrificial enough.

But the more we discussed what we should give, the more disturbed we became. Even problems of growth require a great deal of sacrifice. God was really challenging us to stretch in the area of sacrifice. I remember many long, late night discussions with Mary. Many of those discussions ended in tears.

Logic suggested that there was no way we could give any more money to the church. However, there was more than logic involved. There was the matter of faith. There seemed to be for us two basic questions: what were we going to allow God to channel through us for the building of the new sanctuary and what were we willing to trust God to provide? It sounds simple. Yet it was very hard for us to make a decision.

After much prayer and after many hours of getting in touch with each other's heart and the heart of God, Mary and I made a three year commitment which doubled our giving. It was scary to go from 12% to 24%. The old doubt crept in. What if we couldn't keep our commitment? What if we ruined ourselves financially trying to give this much away? It's very human to question. The important thing is how you deal with questions of doubt. Only faith can drive doubt away. The antidote to doubt is to trust that God can do anything. The Bible defines faith:

> "Now faith is being sure of what we hope for and certain of what we do not see."
>
> (Hebrews 11:1 NIV)

Christ helps fortify us with the courage to dare to doubt our doubts.

The Sense Of Need Is A Gift

GOD DECIDES AND THEN PROVIDES

Only a few days after we signed the commitment card, I received a telephone call from the American Lutheran Church headquarters. Our church had grown rapidly and some great mission and ministry was happening there. The national office of evangelism wanted me to help other congregations. If I agreed to be a consultant, I'd receive $100 a day plus expenses.

That was a double prayer answer for me. First, it would help to pay my new financial commitment to the church. Second, it would give me an opportunity to help struggling churches, which I had wanted to do from the moment I made the decision to enter the seminary. I was thrilled beyond description to see how God was faithfully working in so many extraordinary ways. It was clear that what God decides, God lovingly and generously provides.

INTELLIGENT INVESTING

Money can be a vehicle for accomplishing tremendous things. Many people try to do what's right with their money. I'm not an expert in investments, so I encourage you to consult someone you can trust to give you investment advice. I do believe it's generally good advice not to risk investing money you cannot afford to lose.

In the past, I invested in some high risk ventures. Even though those particular investments were risky, I'd been told they were almost certain to make money and that it wouldn't take long before I'd be receiving literally thousands of dollars every month. I got pretty excited about that!

God Decides
And Then
Provides

Some nights when I went to bed, I had trouble sleeping because I was so busy anticipating our windfall. Mary and I made some big plans for what we'd do with our "pot of gold." It probably won't come as any great surprise that things went from good to bad and then to worse. Eventually I lost the entire investment. The people with whom I'd invested filed bankruptcy. So much for the windfall!

We all would like to get rich quick or have thousands of dollars flowing into our bank accounts. Our nature desires the good things in life. There is nothing wrong with a lot of money as long as the money is managed in such a way as to most honor God and to help other people.

Someone once said to me:

*"I work as much as I can
to make as much as I can
to help as many as I can."*

MONEY CAN MANIPULATE

One of the greatest challenges people with money face is not allowing money to manipulate their family relationships, their health, their time for God, and their time to rest, relax and refresh themselves.

Money places high demands on people. It easily can consume all your energy, all your waking moments and all your thought-life. Money can actually squeeze out God, family, and friends.

A lot of money can give a person a sense of false security, an unhealthy pride, or a feeling of self- sufficiency. If you have it all, it's easy to forget that it was God who gave it all to you. I think that's why Jesus cautioned His beloved people by telling them:

*"I tell you the truth, it is hard for a rich man to enter the
kingdom of heaven. Again I tell you, it is easier for a
camel to go through the eye of a needle than for a rich
man to enter the kingdom of God."*
(Matthew 19:23-24 NIV)

For some, that may mean having a lot of money and for others not having much money at all.

"...seek first His kingdom and His righteousness, and all these things will be given to you as well."
(Matthew 6:33 NIV)

By putting Jesus Christ in first place in our lives, we will succeed beyond our wildest dreams:

"In everything you do, put God first, and He will direct you and crown your efforts with success."
(Proverbs 3:6 Living Bible)

Money can help great dreams come true. Great dreams inspire people. But why do you suppose so many people stop dreaming?

FINANCING GREAT DREAMS

*J*oe bought an automotive center that he'd dreamed about owning ever since he worked there as an errand boy. He invested everything he owned to purchase that business. Only a few weeks after he took over and had everything in place, a raging fire consumed the entire plant.

When I saw the news coverage of the terrible fire, I immediately called Joe to ask how he was. I asked if there was anything I could do or any way I could help. Joe was incredibly positive in the face of such a great loss. He said, "I'm doing fine. My business belongs to the Lord. If God wants to burn it down, then that's what's best."

I was deeply moved. Joe's faith was an encouragement. His dream was big enough to include God. Joe knew he couldn't be successful on his own. He was confident he needed a big God for his big dream. Only God could pull off what needed to be done in the days ahead. In the midst of this tough challenge, Joe was already busy dreaming great dreams.

The Size Of Your
Dream
Is Directly
Related To
The Size Of Your
Sacrifice

HAVING A GOD-SIZED DREAM

I have watched many people, many churches and many corporations stop dreaming great God-inspired dreams because they couldn't figure out a way to finance those great dreams.

When our church went through its severe financial crisis, there were many days I contemplated bringing everything to a screeching halt. As the finances became increasingly inadequate and cash flow was in terrible shape, it would have been easy to react negatively and panic instead of acting positively and pushing ahead.

If I hadn't believed that many people were being helped in so many great ways, I'd have bailed out. There were numerous nights I came home hurting so deeply that I didn't want to continue.

One night as I was pouring out my pain to Christ, this message of encouragement sped across my mind:

THE SIZE OF YOUR DREAM
IS DIRECTLY RELATED
TO THE SIZE OF YOUR SACRIFICE.

In other words, if I was going to dream big dreams, I had better be willing to face enormous sacrifice.

Another thought, similar to the first:

THE SIZE OF YOUR PLAN WILL DETERMINE
THE SIZE OF YOUR PAIN

When I started feeling sorry for myself, it was due in part to my thinking that I was going to get off trouble free. Jesus Christ was crucified for His ultimate dream of salvation and I was complaining about a few months of misery. It's so easy to lose perspective when you're struggling.

A Christian Isn't Isolated From Trouble.

A Christian Is Insulated For Trouble.

DISCIPLINE NUMBER ONE: BIBLE READING AND PRAYER

Some very helpful disciplines enabled me to "keep on keeping on." The first discipline involved my daily devotional and prayers. No one—not even a Christian—is immune from life's problems. Daily Bible reading and prayer time can fortify you to face the storms and struggles of the real world. One person described it this way: " A Christian isn't isolated from trouble. A Christian is insulated for trouble."

Praying and reading the Bible is not a way to get God's attention or to convince God to help you. Prayer and Bible reading is God's activity. It's God's way of attracting our attention. Prayer and Bible study provide us with what we need to live life to the fullest extent possible. One favorite verse I rehearse during tough times is:

"I have come that you may have life, and have it to the fullest."

(John 10:10b NIV)

DISCIPLINE NUMBER TWO: VIGOROUS EXERCISE

The second discipline that helped me find strength during Church of Joy's crisis was regular, vigorous exercise. A universal principle of finance is applicable here. In order to earn money, you have to use money wisely. This is also true of physical fitness. In order to gain stamina and energy, you have to spend energy wisely. If the body is out of shape, the blows from life can severely damage it.

It's not uncommon to see men and women suffer heart attacks, strokes, bleeding ulcers, stress attacks, and other serious illnesses as a result of big problems. Stress breaks down the body's immune system and makes it vulnerable to major illness as well as minor sicknesses like colds and flu.

The Bible gives some wise counsel on getting in shape and staying in shape to live successfully:

"To win the contest, you must deny yourself many things that would keep you from doing your best. An athlete goes to all this trouble just to win a blue ribbon or a silver cup, but we do it for a heavenly reward that never disappears. So I run straight to the goal with purpose in every step. I fight to win. Like an athlete I punish my body, treating it roughly, training it to do what it should, not what it wants to. Otherwise I fear that after enlisting others for the race, I myself might be declared unfit and ordered to stand aside."

(I Corinthians 10:25-27 Living Bible)

*The Size Of Your
Plan
Will Determine
The Size Of Your
Pain*

During those troubled months at Joy, I would wake up many mornings exhausted from a restless night. I'd done enough reading to know it was important for me to get rid of the toxic chemicals that stress had produced in my system. My body needed to be cleaned out and my mind needed to be cleared out.

I didn't want to exercise my weary body, but I did anyway because I knew it would help me. While I exercised and jogged four miles each day, I meditated. This time was invaluable for me to communicate back and forth with God. Often times along the road, amazing solutions to problems flowed into my mind. A helpful little prayer that I commonly prayed as I jogged was:

"Dear Lord, take my mind and think through it. Take my knowledge and set it on fire. Take my heart and fill it with your love. Please love this world through me."

(St. Augustine)

Zig Ziglar calls a bad attitude "stinkin' thinkin'". Our thought life controls our actions and emotions. Focusing on possible bad outcomes only serves to make us miserable. When our attitudes get straightened out and become positive, some beautiful things can happen throughout the day. Expecting that good things will happen increases our enjoyment of life. The Bible tells us that:

"As a person thinks, so is he."

(Proverbs 23:7a KJV)

DISCIPLINE NUMBER THREE: EATING RIGHT

The third discipline that helps tremendously in dealing with problems is eating right. A good diet is essential to maintaining good health. Vitamins and moderate portions of good food are all important to consider in managing your diet.

We've probably all heard the computer-related phrase, "garbage in, garbage out." It seems to apply to diet as well. Creativity, innovation, and strength to find solutions are all impaired by an inadequate diet. Our bodies need to be cared for and treated right. When we respect our bodies, we're rewarded by feeling good.

Even when food tastes flat or the appetite is lost, it's important to eat. Taking care of our bodies really honors God.

"Do you not know that your body is a temple of the Holy Spirit, who is in you, whom you have received from God? You are not your own; you were bought with at a price. Therefore honor God with your body."

(I Corinthians 6:19-20 NIV)

A Problem:
A Challenge
To Think Bigger,
Believe Stronger,
And Live More
Dynamically
Than You Ever
Have Before!!!

DISCIPLINE NUMBER FOUR: REST AND RELAXATION

The fourth discipline I practiced was to get proper rest and relaxation. When we are wrestling with a problem, we often work longer and harder hours with more intensity. "Burnout" is very common for people who are enduring a stormy problem.

Even though I knew I needed to rest properly, I would often work until midnight, and then stumble into bed, too drained of energy even to brush my teeth or to undress. Lack of rest leaves us unable to function effectively in any arena of life. A good warning sign that it's time for rest is when we find ourselves having to work longer on projects that in "good times" could be accomplished quickly.

Rest and peace are elusive in tough times. Yet this is precisely when we most need to be able to make well thought-out, wise decisions.

The need for this discipline became clearest to me after three months of agonizing restless nights. I hadn't been resting well. My muscles became tight and tense. Eventually, my back muscles began to spasm. After only a couple of hours in bed, the pain in my back became so great that I'd have to get up and go into the family room to sit in a chair.

Finally, I got tired of this back pain. One Sunday night, I went up to the altar at church. I asked some people who are very special to me to lay their hands on my back and pray for healing. This was an important moment for me. I needed more than just physical healing. I needed emotional and spiritual healing as well. I was carrying around the weight of the world on my shoulders—well, at least the weight of our congregation—and I was crumbling under its heaviness.

As I knelt at that altar, I felt engulfed by warmth. A penetrating peace helped me to relax more than I had in months. Tears poured down my cheeks, and I asked God to forgive me for trying to play God. I had been trying to solve all the financial problems on my own. I asked my loving Lord to give me a new heart and a new start.

My mind became riveted on the words of Jesus:

> *"Come to me all you who are weary and burdened,*
> *and I will give you rest."*
>
> (Matthew 11:28 NIV)

After meditating on those words, I felt lighter hearted and much more relaxed. That night I went home and fell into a deep sleep lasting eight long, lovely hours. I awoke feeling refreshed and restored.

Always Remember God Is Bigger Than Your Problem

During this ordeal, I did take vacation time, family time and time for my weekly date night with my wife, Mary. Getting away gives you new perspective and insight. When you work too closely with a problem for long periods of time, you become more a part of the problem than the solution.

Even tough athletic contests have time-outs, half-times, and breaks. My friend, if you are in need of some rest and relaxation, let's covenant together to "let go and let God," right now. We'll stop doing God's work on our power and start doing God's work on God's power. Let's take a break and relax.

DISCIPLINE NUMBER FIVE: POSITIVE INFLOW

The fifth discipline helpful to me was reading positive, faith-building, hope-producing books, articles and magazines. My mind needed to be saturated with encouraging, inspiring words.

When times are tough, it's easy to get down or discouraged or depressed. It doesn't take very long for a person who is suffering to lose perspective about life. What can be done about such a degenerative condition?

I made a conscious decision that the positive inflow would exceed the negative input in my life. Whenever I was in the car, I listened to positive Christian messages by Drs. Norman Vincent Peale, Robert Schuller, Lloyd Ogilvie, Charles Swindoll, Dennis Waitley and several others. My thoughts needed to be lifted out of the *ruts* of nursing my own regrets to the *possibilities* of new rewards and opportunities.

*Loving And
Being Loved By
God Is The Most
Important
Decision You Will
Ever Make*

As I listened to these positive people, I heard anew that every problem is filled with potential. A problem is not necessarily an enemy. A problem is a challenge to think bigger, believe stronger and live more dynamically than you ever have before.

Jesus took the problem of the cross and transformed it into a cross of victory. As the old Gospel song says, "If you can't bear the cross, you can't wear the crown." Someone told me that trouble gives you tread to run to God. I was most assuredly re-treaded as I filled my mind with invigorating inspiration and hope.

It's easy to forget there's any "good news" when you're surrounded with bad news. Reading positive books and literature helps you remember that God is bigger than your problem. There is nothing that we will face on any given day that with God's help we cannot handle.

DISCIPLINE NUMBER SIX: LET GOD LOVE YOU

The sixth helpful discipline was to let God love me. So often I see people make an enemy out of God when they need God's friendship most. When trouble comes, the tendency is to push God out of our life. Willingness to let God love us is evidence that we have surrendered all of our problems, as well as our potential possibilities, to God. God's great love is unconditional and non-judgmental.

Friends, family, work associates, pastors and others are appointed to communicate to us how much God loves and is pleased with us. Their gentle words or hugs or just their presence form the riverbed God uses for the flow of hope, happiness and healing. The natural reaction to want to do it on our own needs to be changed.

Problems never leave you where they find you. You will always have decisions to make. A decision to be open to God's love touching your life will make you better. A decision to run from God or to try to turn God off will make you bitter. Choosing to allow yourself to love and be loved by God is one of the most important decisions you will ever make.

NEVER QUIT

Two extremely powerful words I learned as I discovered how to finance great dreams were: *NEVER QUIT!* It's always too soon to quit!

I loved my daughter Shawn's response to me one day following a race she participated in. I asked her, "Well, honey, did you win?"

She responded enthusiastically, saying, "No, Dad, I didn't win, but I didn't quit!"

God has given each person an extraordinary capacity to think unlimited thoughts, to come up with bright new ideas. As my mother reminds me from time to time: "When you think you've thought of or tried everything, always remember you haven't."

Psychologists tell us that the average person uses only a small percentage of their brain capacity. Whenever you have an unsolvable problem, decide to ask God to help you think bigger and deeper and wider than you have ever thought before.

One day as I was working diligently, trying to solve our church's financial crisis, a new idea occurred to me. I had never personally met with any of the executive officers of Lutheran Brotherhood, the company I was trying to convince to refinance our church.

After some phone calls, I arranged for a meeting in Minneapolis with one of the officers. I flew there to present to him our need and the tremendous future our church would have if this need could be met. Because he was so impressed with the story of Church of Joy, he was very influential some time later in helping us secure our refinancing package. After four rejections, the answer the fifth time was yes!

DREAM BIG ENOUGH TO DREAM ABOUT SERVING

In finding finances to enable great dreams to become reality, many people dream too small. Big dreams inspire people. Fear of failure reduces many giant oak tree dreams to the size of an acorn. People are looking for a sure thing. So often the desire to play it safe seems more important than the desire to soar. The truth is that the more risky the dream is and the bigger it becomes, the more likely it will get off the ground and become a reality. Always remember that the essence of faith is risk.

"Dream Big"
Dream
God-Sized
Dreams

People with money are not looking for mediocrity. They are looking for the best. I'm not suggesting that a dream has to dazzle people to happen. I am saying that if your dream can help people in a greater way than they have been helped before, if you can fill a need that no one else has been able to fill, if you can heal a hurt that no one else can heal, your dream will most likely generate the money required to make it happen. *MAKING GREAT DREAMS HAPPEN IS NOT A MATTER OF SELLING. IT IS A MATTER OF SERVING.*

Here is how I am personally applying what I am sharing with you. There is only one Christian four-year liberal arts college in the state of Arizona. I have a dream to help launch one of the most dynamic Christian colleges in America right here in Phoenix, Arizona. It's already attracting many of the people and resources necessary to make it happen.

I have another dream of building a "Disney World for Senior Citizens" where seniors can hardly wait to get up each morning to live out the day with enjoyment and delight. Plans, resources and people are now coming together to make that a reality.

Making Great Dreams Happen Is Not A Matter Of Selling - It's A Matter Of Serving

BE REALISTIC IN YOUR DREAMING

Dreams require enormous dedication, determination, and discipline. Include God in making big dreams happen. God's mighty and miraculous work can literally make the dream come true.

Realism is an essential ingredient in the foundational financial planning and development of any great dreams. We so often hear someone say, "Be realistic." It is wise to look at reality. A person needs to count the cost and list the problems that the dream will produce.

> *"Suppose one of you wants to build a tower. Will he not first sit down and estimate the cost to see if he has enough money to complete it? For if he lays the foundation and is not able to finish it, everyone who sees it will ridicule him, saying, 'This fellow began to build and was not able to finish.'"*

(Luke 14:28-30 NIV)

When I present an idea, I talk about its strengths and weaknesses. But the launching of a dream happens when you make a commitment to face each and every obstacle head on and confidently decide to overcome them all.

What separates a dream that becomes a reality from a dream that is simply "pie in the sky" are detailed plans, timetables and follow-through assignments. Dreams don't just happen. People make them happen with God's help.

When You Think You've Thought Of Everything, Always Remember You Haven't

THE FOUR B'S

Don't be timid or tentative about your dreams. Apply these four B's to allow your dreams to unfold:

1. Be bold.
2. Be enthusiastic.
3. Be expectant.
4. Be committed to hard work, discipline and sacrifice.

As you draw your dream out on paper, share it freely with others. Concentrate on developing every detail of your dream including when, where, how, why and who. The more concrete you are, the greater the receptivity will be.

Dreams Don't Just Happen – People Make Them Happen With God's Help

UNFOLDING A DREAM

For the past five years, I have had a dream to build a Christian Living and Leadership Center. Right now I am in the process of doing the following steps:

1. Inspiring key people with this God-inspired idea.
2. Determining all the needs that this beautiful building can meet.
3. Photographing people who will benefit from this dream to produce an appealing multi-media presentation to be shown to potential supporters.
4. Getting unique, one-of-a-kind architectural drawings developed and distributed.
5. Requesting that a scale model be built and an attractive rendering painted.
6. Planning a financial campaign for erecting this building debt free.
7. Committing myself to the dedication, discipline and sacrifice necessary to make it happen.
8. Trusting God's help more, without which nothing would ever happen.

I urge you to dare to dream great dreams. God encourages all of us to dream, saying:

"The people without a vision perish."
(Proverbs 29:18a KJV)

An unselfish dream designed to lift up and care for people is like a precious jewel. Handle all God-inspired dreams with care and with prayer. A God-inspired dream enables people to become winners. When they win, you win.

RAISING MONEY

ASK FOR IT

One of the most talked about benevolent gifts in some Lutheran circles was the gift given by John Green, a Lutheran, to Dr. Robert Schuller's ministry. The gift was a piece of property worth several million dollars. Whenever I heard Lutherans talking about it, I heard them say, "Why did John give this property to Dr. Schuller's ministry and not to a Lutheran church or organization?"

Dr. Schuller's wonderful answer to this question was, "Mr. Green gave it to my ministry because I asked for it."

That is the key principle in raising money: *"ASK FOR IT."* There are two reasons why most people find it difficult to ask for money. The first reason is fear—specifically, fear of rejection. The second reason is pride. Asking for financial help from someone else is an admission that you need their help. You're admitting that you cannot do it alone.

OVERCOMING THE FEAR OF REJECTION

The fear of rejection is real. One of the toughest lessons I had to learn in raising money was that a 'no' in response to an invitation for financial participation and support is not a personal rejection. It is not a put-down of me.

The Best Way To Raise Money Is To Ask For It

The first few times I asked someone for money, I trembled inside. I will never forget when I was seeking to raise $10,000 for a Gospel team ministry. I drove 300 miles to the first of four pre-arranged appointments. I was a nervous wreck by the time I arrived.

My approach was going to be non-directive. It ended up being so non-directive that they really didn't know why I came to visit them. 22 hours and 650 miles later, I had raised $100, which just covered the expenses of the trip. Not surprisingly, I decided I wanted to get out of fundraising.

I hadn't yet learned that I wasn't raising this money for myself. I was not begging for my own financial gain. The mission God had called me to accomplish needed to be financed, and the finances were to be provided through God's people. This was a very important discovery for me. It actually helped me turn fear into faith. It gave me new confidence and courage to "ask again."

Learn How To Turn Fear Into Faith

ADMITTING YOU CAN'T DO IT ALONE

The matter of pride is more difficult. We like to feel self-sufficient and to have a sense of self-made success. Actually, admitting the need for help opens the door to lasting success.

It's true that "people who need people are the luckiest people in the world." Most great accomplishments have required the support and assistance of many people. Even God enlisted the help of a person—Mary—to bring Jesus Christ into the world.

BUILD FRIENDSHIPS

One of the primary rules in raising money is to build friendships. Build bridges. Build meaningful relationships. By doing this, you will win the right to be heard.

In 1985, some good friends of our family, Wayne and Sheila Wright, invited us to a week of celebration at the Dominion in San Antonio, Texas. During one of our conversations, Wayne told me about an outstanding woman who lived in Phoenix, Arizona. Her home was located on the prestigious Biltmore Golf Course. Wayne suggested that if I ever got a chance, I should stop by to visit with her. I jotted down her name in a little notebook I always carry with me.

You Can Never Raise Money Without First Raising People

A few weeks passed. One evening I decided to drive to the Biltmore Golf Course to see if I could find Wayne's friend. I'd been told she had the largest home on the golf course.

On my way there, I remember feeling apprehensive. Then the thought occurred to me, "What's the worst thing that could happen?" Well, the worst thing would be that this person wouldn't want to talk to me.

As I arrived in the area, I spotted an enormous house alongside a private road. As I got closer, I saw a high wrought iron fence surrounding the property. The house itself was one of the most beautiful I'd ever seen. I wondered how I'd get inside to the driveway, to say nothing of how I'd get inside the house to visit personally with the owner.

I pulled the car up as close as I could get it and noticed that the main gate was open. I speculated about what might happen if I drove in. Would security guards arrest me? I could see myself calling my wife to bail me out of jail.

I decided to drive in. I parked my car and proceeded cautiously by foot past some large, interesting fountains. By now I could see the front door, which was by no means ordinary. It was almost as large as the whole front of my house. I pushed the lighted doorbell.

The door opened, and standing before me was a petite, attractive woman. I introduced myself. Then I explained that I was there to meet this person that my friends in Texas had spoken of so highly. She identified herself as being that person. She smiled and invited me to come in.

I decided I could relax. It had taken some courage to walk up to a stranger's house. But no one had done nor said anything terrible to me. So, my plan was to transform this stranger into a friend.

I spent the next 45 minutes touring the house and talking with her in the reading room. I was impressed! My friend had been right. This woman was an outstanding gift of God. When I learned that she was a Lutheran who'd grown up in Iowa, why of course that made her seem even more radiant!

God Is Full Of
Good Ideas

As we talked, I discovered that she was planning a major benefit golf tournament to raise money for locating missing children. That sounded like a great project. I offered to help her. As things worked out, our church donated $500 seed money as a Father's Day gift, honoring all the fathers in our church. I was invited to serve as the chaplain for this important event.

In the months and years that followed my visit to her house, Helen Rae Smith gave many special gifts to Community Church of Joy because she appreciated our mission and ministry. At Joy, we celebrated together and thanked God for this generosity.

GOD IS FULL OF GOOD IDEAS

Remember that God is neither "broke," nor limited to our money-raising ideas. God is full of good ideas. A couple of years ago an exciting experience taught me that you never say no to a great God-given idea because you don't have the money. *What God decides, God always provides.*

One sunny spring Sunday after church, a woman came to me and introduced herself. She asked whether we were looking for an intern pastor. She wanted to discuss the possibility for her son-in-law.

I'd considered the idea, but the church's finances prohibited my pursuing it very far. Still, I wasn't going to cut off the conversation. I needed the help and I really wanted to give seminary students the opportunity to be a part of our dynamic church. That would help all of us to grow.

We continued the conversation by agreeing to meet together the following week to discuss in greater detail the possibility of an intern at Joy. Don't make the mistake of closing off a new idea before you've thought it through or because there seems to be no way to pay for it!

I met with the woman and we talked some more about her son-in law coming to Community of Joy that fall as an intern. Showing me a wedding picture of Tim and Jan Wright, she assured me that son-in-law Tim was top drawer material. As we visited further, the excitement grew.

Still, I felt I had to be honest with her. I said, "I'd love to have

Tim serve as our intern this fall. I really need help and I believe Tim could develop and learn some important things about working in a church as well.

"The main obstacle right at this moment is obtaining the money. If you'll work with me in getting the finances needed, I'll pursue it."

We worked together and by that fall we had raised the $15,000 we needed. This happy story has a very happy ending. Tim, Jan and their two children, Alycia and Michael, finished the internship with highest commendations and returned to full-time ministry at Joy following the final year of seminary. If I had let money dictate my decision, Joy's ministry would have suffered.

Never Ask Anyone To Do Anything You Yourself Are Not Willing To Do

GENEROUS PEOPLE LOOK AT MONEY DIFFERENTLY

I have found that the people who argue, fuss, and stew most over money matters in the church often are those who give the least. That's why we made the commitment to tithe one of the requirements to becoming a church leader. Certainly God commands it. Leaders lead not only with words but also by the example of their lives. The Bible says:

"These people come near to me with their mouth and honor me with their lips, but their hearts are far from me."

(Isaiah 29:13 NIV)

An important rule to remember in fund raising is never to ask anyone to do anything you yourself are not willing to do. I'm not suggesting you can't ask for a million dollars if you aren't willing to give a million dollars first. But if you are asking someone to be generous and sacrificial, you must be willing to take the first step in being generous and sacrificial.

This is one problem I see in the church and in other fund raising projects. People with little or no commitment are recruited to go out and ask for a gift or a pledge. Their hearts just aren't in it. Consequently, their presentation is less than enthusiastic. When fund raising, always try to match generous people with people from whom you are seeking a generous response.

People Give To People Not To Projects Or Programs

PEOPLE GIVE TO PEOPLE

When it gets right down to it, people give to people. You can have the greatest cause, project, building program or plan in the world, but if people presenting the need aren't 100% enthused about their own commitment, they won't be warmly received and the gift will range from minimal to nothing at all.

A friendship needs to be established before a gift of money is requested. The rewards of patiently and lovingly taking the time to be a genuine friend are great. An age old truth needs to be applied: "We need to win the right to be heard."

For most of his life, Wayne Wright hadn't had much time for ministers. He loved to give them a rough time and verbally tussle with them. He wasn't much of a churchgoer, but he went just often enough to satisfy his wife.

Before we knew each other, Wayne's wife, Sheila, showed up at our church one Sunday for the first time. That particular day we announced that we were having a rummage sale to raise funds for a mission organization.

Sheila left a message at the church office the next morning, offering a solar panel for the rummage sale. I happened to see the note and I decided to set up an appointment to meet the Wright family.

When Wayne heard that the preacher was coming, he asked Sheila what time I'd be leaving. She told him I'd be gone by 8:30 p.m. He said, "Fine, I'll be home at 9."

I enjoyed my visit with Sheila. We talked about the Midwest where we both grew up and about her husband, whom she admired very much. It was unusual for me to stay longer than 30 or 45 minutes, and we had a two-hour visit. In the midst of our conversation, Wayne walked into the house.

When I saw Wayne come in, I enthusiastically greeted him and said, "Your wife has been telling me what an incredible guy you are. How did you become so successful?"

Wayne answered me politely. All the while, Sheila was worrying that her husband might throw me out or at the very least try to intimidate me.

Our conversation continued and I discovered that Wayne appreciated the works of Norman Vincent Peale. I'd just returned from spending a week with Dr. Peale in New York, so I was able to talk firsthand about someone Wayne admired.

I enjoyed talking with Wayne and evidently he enjoyed talking with me, because we visited for another two hours! Before I left, he invited me to have breakfast with him the following week.

Not long after our breakfast meeting, Wayne started coming to church. Over time, we developed a great friendship which culminated some years later when I had the privilege of baptizing him in the Jordan River during our trip to the Holy Land. The friendship had been established. The right to be heard had been established.

God exceeded my greatest expectations when, on the Dedication Sunday of our new sanctuary, Wayne and Sheila gave $15,000 toward the beautiful fountains located in Joy's courtyard. Friendship was the motivation. When friendship developed, loving generosity poured out.

SUPPORT YOUR SUPPORTERS

In raising money, it is crucial to develop and maintain a prospect list. These prospects need to be contacted on a regular basis. I've developed a special card file that consists of members of Joy and also non-members who visit our church.

Every congregation member has friends, relatives or acquaintances who are good potential supporters of our ministry. These people are identified and placed on our mailing list.

You Never Have A Money Problem It Is Always An Idea Problem

Our church has a weekly newspaper. We send this publication to about twice the number on our membership mailing list. By regular communication of the plans, dreams, goals, and exciting ministry, people are kept current with the needs. During the past few years more than a quarter million dollars has been given each year to our ministry by friends and acquaintances of Joy who are not members.

It's important to be creative and innovative in raising money. Financial wizards tell us that we never have a money problem— it's always an idea problem. My staff brainstorms regularly. It's an enjoyable time.

RAISING MONEY PERSONALLY

Raising money can be done professionally and also personally. A loving, giving person facing a crisis and needing money to help out will almost always receive it.

I think it's important to take some of the principles mentioned earlier in this chapter and apply them to our personal situation. For example, the decision to share your need takes a lot of humility. If you've never admitted you needed help, don't be surprised if no one has helped you. When you're willing to admit you need help, you'll be amazed how people respond.

Blessings Can Boomerang!

CAST YOUR BREAD UPON THE WATERS

A Biblical principle also operates here. It is called the "casting your bread upon the waters" principle:

"Cast your bread upon the waters, for after many days you will find it again."

(Ecclesiastes 11:1 NIV)

In simple language, people reap what they sow. A generous person reaps generosity.

When I go to the hospital to visit, the people with the most flowers, cards, and visitors are usually warm, caring people. Blessings can boomerang!

A word of caution about fundraising. It is essential that money not become the ultimate goal. Money is not an end in itself. Money is simply a means to an end—the end being loving, honoring, obeying and enjoying God as well as God's beautiful people. Raising money for money's sake is always disappointing. Raising money for mission's sake is always rewarding.

Life is meant to be joyfully rewarding. But there's something that actually can steal joy away from us. It can destroy marriages, beautiful plans, self-worth, and personal dignity. That something is DEBT. Let's take a look at how to overcome debt and experience the "joy of being debt free."

THE JOY OF BEING DEBT FREE

DEBT CAN ROB YOU OF DIGNITY

Debt can be very dehumanizing. Community Church of Joy's debt nearly destroyed a dynamic ministry as well as an enthusiastic minister. I learned firsthand what is meant by the Biblical warning:

> *"Let no debt be outstanding, except the continuing debt to love one another..."*
>
> (Romans 13:8a NIV)

I'll never forget the severe lecture the bank president delivered to me and to the president of our congregation. Essentially, he said, "For God's sake, for the sake of the future ministry, and for the sake of all the families of Joy, get your financial act together!"

This banker talked tough to us because he loved us and supported the ministry of our church. He deeply cared about our future success, beyond its financial implications for his bank.

A PROMISE

That night, I got down on my knees and promised God that

our church would never again borrow for buildings, programs, staff or for anything. I would trust God and not financial institutions for the money we needed.

Debt
Can Rob You
Of Dignity

I don't want to create the impression that all borrowing for everyone in all circumstances is bad. Most people could never buy a house without a 15 or 30 year mortgage. Many businesses need to borrow to make more money. But before you borrow, make absolutely sure there's no other alternative and that you have the cash flow to adequately manage the debt.

DEVELOP ALTERNATIVES TO BORROWING

I believe that for churches there are other alternatives to borrowing. For mission-oriented organizations, the money received needs to be used to provide adequate staff, necessary programs and supplies to maintain the ministry. When we borrow, we are taking from the ministry to pay for the debt. The money lost in interest doesn't benefit the mission at all. In fact, instead of developing resources, it drains them.

In Chapter Six, we read about financing great dreams. Any exciting dream is attractive. I don't believe it's necessary to borrow to build. It takes more blood, sweat, tears and hard work up front, but the reward comes when the ministry can sail smoothly along debt free.

Some might say, "It's impossible not to borrow!" The truth is, it's impossible only if you decide it is. We all have a tendency to take the path of least resistance. What I am suggesting is the roughest way to go, but the rewards of being debt free are tremendous.

START SMART

I respect our Lutheran Church organization, but I question the way it handles newly-formed congregations.

To start a church, the headquarters scouts a piece of land in an area of great potential growth. Next they erect the first building on that property. Then, just as the new congregation is trying to get started by recruiting members, they inherit a debt of $250,000, $500,000 or even more. So, before the congregation even has 100 members, they have an enormous debt load.

When I arrived at Joy, the church had already accumulated a debt of $272,000. That was a heavy burden for our infant organization. It takes many churches ten years or more to recover from that kind of indebtedness.

It seems to me that established congregations near the area where the new church will be planted should be challenged to raise up-front the necessary funds for building and developing the new church. Thousands of churches across America are located in areas that won't be building new churches. They could be of tremendous help by agreeing to include infant congregations in their benevolence budgets.

One of the problems that needs to be overcome is the over-protection of a congregation's territory. Many churches don't like to see new churches established close to them because they see them as unwanted competition. This unhealthy jealousy is counterproductive. Christians aren't adversaries. They're on the same team. Great things can happen when we don't care who gets the credit and are willing to work together.

Additional ways to avoid high debt start-ups in churches include placing a gifted developer or fund raiser in the community to challenge people with a vision for mission to generously give. Encourage people with financial resources to commit themselves to being a "midwife" for new spiritual birth and development. Still another way is to challenge fraternal insurance companies to match the money raised for the new church.

Another idea is to get the investors to buy the land and buildings and lease them to the church for 99 years at $1.00 a year. Still another idea is leasing shopping center space for the church that would provide visibility, accessibility, parking, and all the other ingredients required for successful marketing. There are dozens more ideas, and God's innovation and creativity will inspire ideas that work.

You Are Called From Convenience To Commitment

MAKE THE DECISION NOT TO BORROW

My wife, Mary, and I decided to enjoy the reward of a commitment to being debt free. We still have a long way to go. However, the decision not to borrow to build an addition to our house that we both earnestly wanted was the first step.

There were many reasons why we needed a new addition. Furthermore, the equity in our home had risen high enough to qualify us for a second mortgage. As we carefully planned this new beautiful space, we sometimes dreamed out loud, sharing with one another our excitement about the addition.

One morning, Mary and I were having breakfast together. I asked her, "Why are we borrowing more money? We're just putting a heavier load on our monthly payments that will cause a constant strain on our finances."

We agreed we could make it, but why were we even considering heaping more debt load onto an already heavy responsibility? Many people live in such a way that they are always at or beyond their maximum financial limit. Then when something goes wrong, when someone gets sick, or when something needs to be replaced, there's sheer panic.

Why do we do that to ourselves? It reminds me of a coat rack we used to have. The rack had a wooden peg sticking out to one side. When we walked into the house, we'd hang coats, ties, umbrellas, handbags and other things on this peg. Well, one day we loaded this peg down with too many things and it broke. That's the image I had of our finances. Loading ourselves down with debt may cause us one day to break.

BEING DEBT FREE IS AN ATTITUDE

Being debt free is an attitude of patient waiting, perseverance, planning and saving. It's not instant gratification. It's not the "buy now, pay later" mentality that has really become the lifestyle of our day. That lifestyle is built on an eggshell foundation. There's no substance to it.

DEBT CAN KILL DREAMS

Now I'm a positive thinker, not a "gloom and doom" personality. But when we have to borrow money to pay back money we've already borrowed, we can be assured this borrowing spells disaster.

That's what America is doing. Unless the decision is made to become a debt-free society instead of a debt-oriented society, America will be bankrupt. There will be no money for all of the important things we take for granted today.

Each and every week I observe what debt does to marriages, families, and friendships. The pressure debt puts on marriages often ends in bitter divorce. As couples come into my office, many have grown to hate one another over debt. Recently I saw a family shattered, even requiring hospitalization in a psychiatric unit, over demeaning debt. I have seen friends fight and sometimes even sue each other over debt.

TEN STEPS TO ENJOY BEING DEBT FREE

What can be done individually, in a marriage, with the family and with others to deal with debt positively? Let's look at ten important steps:

1. MAKE A COMMITMENT

Make a commitment to be debt free. Once you have decided to be debt free, you re-orient your entire financial management around this decision. A commitment to be debt free requires sacrifice.

Debt Never Leaves You Where It Finds You – It Either Makes You Better Or It Makes You Bitter

One of my favorite stories about sacrifice involves a chicken, a pig and a cow. One day these three farm animal friends were walking around the barnyard. It was a perfect day for a picnic.

The chicken clucked out, "How about having a picnic out under the shade trees in the pasture?"

The cow mooed, "A picnic sounds like a great idea."

Then the pig grunted, "Let's all bring something to eat that we can share with each other." That seemed like a great idea.

Soon the chicken cackled, "I'll brings some eggs to eat."

Next the cow offered, "I'll bring some milk to drink." Then she turned to the pig and suggested, "Why don't you bring the ham?"

This elicited a squealing response from the pig. "That's easy for *you* to say. For you to bring eggs and milk is only a contribution, but for me to bring ham requires total sacrifice!"

To become debt free requires that a person decide to manage their money, not for convenience, but from sacrificial commitment.

2. START SAVING NOW

Start saving a portion of your income. I recently read that there's a growing number of American families who spend 10% or 20% more each week than they earn.

Earn It Before You Spend It

After graduating from college, I considered myself a learned man. I certainly wasn't a genius but I was capable of figuring things out. Yet somehow I couldn't figure out how I could deposit $500 or $1000 in Mary's and my account one day and get a notice the next day stating that I'd already dipped into our instant credit reserve.

I was really happy in those days to get my paycheck and be able to put it into our checking account. After making the deposit, I'd cheerfully bounce home and announce to my wife that we were going out to dinner because we had some extra money. After all, I'd just put hundreds of dollars into our account.

Then Mary would say to me, "We don't have enough money to go out to dinner tonight."

I'd snap back, "What do you mean we don't have enough money? Didn't you hear me when I said I filled up our account again?"

What happened was that I'd already committed the money I brought home before I'd even earned it to the car payment, the new furniture, the house payment, the clothes I had charged. How depressing! Nothing was left to do anything new. I'd spent today's money yesterday. That's when I learned the advantage of savings.

3. EARN IT BEFORE YOU SPEND IT

Develop the patience to wait until you actually have the money before you spend it. So many promised raises or bonuses simply go up in smoke. When you actually get the money in hand, use it wisely.

At the end of 1984, I was promised a significant raise beginning in 1985. Mary and I went for our evening walks and talked about what we'd do with the new money that had been promised. Well, our planning didn't last long. When 1985 came, the church entered its financial crisis and not only did I not receive a raise, I took a 25% cut along with the rest of the staff.

Now if Mary and I had purchased the backyard spa we wanted on the promise of that raise, we'd have been in deep trouble. It's wise to practice patience in moving ahead financially.

4. SPEND ONLY THE INTEREST, NOT THE SUBSTANCE

Agree to spend only the interest you earn on financial investments, inheritances, or special gifts. Leave the principal alone. Then you'll always have money coming in. If you blow the source, you also blow the security.

A friend of our family's received $100,000 from an insurance settlement. If our friend had put that money in a savings plan of some kind, it would have paid at least $10,000 a year. Instead, this friend started spending the principal. It didn't take long before the $100,000 was completely gone. Now our friend is struggling to earn enough money to pay for normal living expenses. That $100,000 could have provided some helpful security. Always remember, when you get extra money, invest it. You can spend the interest, but leave the principal alone.

5. BE CREATIVE

Be creative in generating new sources of income. Invest your talents and time wisely. They are actually the best assets you have. Certainly, if they're properly managed, you'll have a more than adequate supply of income.

My family was invited to be guests at a lovely horse ranch in Wickenburg, Arizona. During our morning horseback ride, I asked the owner how he became so successful. As he talked, it became clear that he had been very creative in his personal finances.

At one point, he had a job during the day as a workman for a large corporation, earning an average wage. Wanting to get ahead, he realized that this job would never give him the financial rewards he wanted for himself and his family.

So he started cleaning bathrooms in a restaurant at night. This gave him a little extra money. Soon another restaurant hired him to clean its bathrooms. It wasn't long before he had more bathrooms to clean than he could handle. He soon had to hire someone to help him. He got more bathroom cleaning jobs and he hired more help.

Pretty soon, he had a successful bathroom cleaning business. He quit his other job because the bathroom cleaning business took all his time and paid much higher wages. After building up his cleaning business, he sold it for several million dollars. He was financially successful. We can do it, too. We need to be creative with all of our time and talents.

*God
Delights
In Our
Delights*

6. IMAGINE BEING DEBT FREE

Imagine how fantastic it would be to be debt free. Picture the joy. Add up the money you are now using to service debt and think about what you could enjoy with it that you are not now enjoying.

The Bible encourages us to imagine big:

"Now to Him who is able to do immeasurably more than all we ask or imagine, according to His power that is at work within us."

(Ephesians 3:20 NIV)

Imagination is one of God's greatest gifts to us. My imagination was thoroughly stimulated recently when I went to Epcot Center in Orlando, Florida. I brought home a replica of the mascot whose name is "Figment." Figment sits in the bay window in front of my office desk at church. He is a constant reminder to use my imagination to the fullest extent possible.

Take a few minutes away from reading this book and join me now in imagining what it would be like to be debt free. It feels good, doesn't it?

7. ASK FOR GOD'S HELP

Ask God to help. God will give wisdom and guidance that we never had before. God desires us to be free to enjoy life even more than we desire it. It's exciting to know that *God actually delights in our delights.* God made this promise:

"Call upon me and I will answer you and tell you great and unsearchable things you do not know."
(Jeremiah 33:3 NIV)

God is on call 24 hours a day, ready to help us even before we ask. In fact, I believe God even prompts us to ask. We don't need to use spiritual language nor well- structured prayers. Just say, "God help me. Thank you. Amen."

8. GENEROUSLY GIVE

Generously give away at least 10% of what you are earning. This is really God's plan of economics that the Bible describes in Luke 6:38 (NIV):

> *"Give, and it will be given unto you. A good measure, pressed down, shaken together and running over, will be poured into your lap. For with the measure you use, it will be measured to you."*

See what happened when some people who had nothing ended up receiving everything they needed.

> *"Out of the most severe trial, then overflowing joy and their extreme poverty welled up in rich generosity."*
> (2 Corinthians 8:2 NIV)

That can happen to us, too. No matter what our financial condition is, generosity is an essential ingredient to financial success.

*Turn Financial
Sores
Into Financial
Soars*

Two years ago when I visited the Holy Land, I traveled to the Dead Sea. The reason that body of water is unattractive, with no living thing surviving in it, is that it's a "taker" and not a "giver." Water flows in, but none flows out.

Don't have a "dead sea" mentality with your finances. Have a "mighty flowing river" mentality.

9. START RIGHT NOW

Every successful motivational lecturer I've ever heard has said, "Do it now!" My dad keeps telling me, "It's important to begin right away." That's sound advice. Schedule time today to look over your financial situation and begin developing plans to operating your finances with a debt-free mentality.

Eight years ago I said I needed to start exercising regularly. There was a myriad of excuses for my not getting started. It was too hot. I was too tired. I was too stiff or sore. My schedule was too demanding.

One day I finally said, "I'm going to exercise right now." And I did. Exercise has been part of my daily routine ever since that day. I feel better and I'm healthier.

One person said, "Beginning is half done." Begin right now planning a "new beginning" for your finances. The Bible urges us:

> "*Choose for yourselves* this day *whom you will serve...*"
>
> (Joshua 24:15 NIV)

The time is *now. You got it—now get at it!*

Be And Feel
Brand New

10. SEEK GOOD COUNSEL

Seek good counsel. Go to your banker or a financial advisor and tell that person you've made a decision to be a debt-free person. Find out what they recommend.

How's this for straight talk from the Bible?

"Plans fail for lack of counsel, but with many advisors they succeed."

(Proverbs 15:22 NIV)

Successful people surround themselves with people smarter than they are. They seek wise counsel. People who come to the church with a counseling need are intelligent people. They have discovered that counseling can help them become bigger and better people.

BE AND FEEL BRAND NEW

By following these ten steps, you can begin to be and to feel like a new person. One of my favorite stories about feeling new and free is about eagles learning to fly.

Live Beyond Borrowing

The mother eagle has long prepared for the wonderful day when her little eaglets hatched. During their earliest days, the mother regularly feeds these precious creatures and provides for all of their comfort, protection, and care.

As the baby eagles begin to grow and develop, soft feathers which had lined their nest are pulled out, exposing thorny branches. Feedings are more sporadic. The mother eagle wants to prepare her young to become what they were created to be—mighty soaring eagles.

Flying lessons must be scary for the little birds. They're pushed out of the nest and as they flutter, they're caught on the pinions of their mother's strong wings. Soon the birds are flying.

As they fly higher and stronger, they discover the jet stream, which propels them into a mightier and more magnificent flight than they imagined possible.

LIVE BEYOND BORROWING

You now have read how to live beyond borrowing. You can be a bigger and better person than you may have believed possible. A debtor is really a slave. Debt tells you what to do, when to do it, and how. Deadlines are imposed on you by the lender and you are living by their rules and regulations.

Have The Guts
To Leave The
Ruts Of Debt

It's demoralizing when our hard labor today already has a claim on it. What we're earning isn't even ours. We end up living to please our money master instead of pleasing God, our family, and our loved ones. The Bible emphasizes:

"It is for freedom that Christ has set us free. Stand firm then, and do not let yourselves be burdened again by a yoke of slavery."

(Galations 5:1 NIV)

Life Without Obstacles Leads Nowhere

God really wants each one of us to be free...free to laugh, free to celebrate, free to enjoy, free to dream, free to hope, free to speak, and free to give.

Dare to be debt free. Again, it's really a matter of having a positive attitude toward a debt-free life. Consider all the advantages. It's pretty convincing.

Join me in encouraging friends, family, senators, congressmen and congresswomen, governors, pastors, community leaders, doctors, farmers, business men and women, homemakers, labor union officials, and bankers that living beyond borrowing is a wonderful way to live. It's a key to living our life as beautifully as God originally planned it for us.

HAVE THE GUTS TO LEAVE THE RUTS OF DEBT

This is a major commitment. It takes guts to leave the ruts of debt. I invite you to dream with me. In order to get out of the debt trap, it takes all the creativity, innovation, and new ideas we can possibly muster up.

Let's expand our present horizons. Let's transcend the normal limits and see how we can succeed with this "dream come true" of being debt free.

"With man this is impossible, but with God all things are possible."

(Matthew 19:26 NIV)

CREATIVE FINANCES

CREATIVITY EXHIBITS THE VERY BEST OF GOD

Just think how creative God was when the world was being created! God must have had a "blast" thinking up and creating animals like the giraffe and the hippopotamus and the orang-utan. Creating beautiful sunsets must have made God radiate with warm satisfaction.

Finally, with creative juices really flowing, God created humankind, which we are told filled God with indescribable delight and joy. After finishing this creative world—every plant and planet, every animal, the stars, the sun and moon, wonderful humankind, and everything else—God said, "It is very good." (Genesis 1:31 paraphrased)

Creativity exhibits the very best of God's creation. That is why these seven negative words—*we've never done it that way before*—are so destructive to God's intention and design for life. The Bible encourages:

> *"Now your attitudes and thoughts must all be*
> *constantly changing for the better. Yes, you must be a*
> *new and different person."*
>
> (Ephesians 4:23-24 Living Bible)

*Creativity
Exhibits The
Very Best Of
God*

FINANCIAL CREATIVITY

This encouragement for creativity applies to all areas of our lives, including our finances. Many times throughout the years, my spendable income has been far less than my spending desires.

One night years ago, when I took my date out for dinner, I discovered that I was low on cash. The restaurant was a low price hamburger stand. When I realized my financial situation, I asked my date (now my wife) if she was willing to split a hamburger with me. She was. Since then, we've shared a meal almost every time we've gone out to eat. This creative idea has helped us financially and physically. We stay physically fit as well as financially fit.

Most nice restaurants serve too much food for one person to consume. By the time we've finished the meal, we've also passed our comfort zone. We walk away feeling stuffed and the enjoyment of the dining experience is diminished. We can almost cut the bill in half when meals are shared. Think about it the next time you go out to eat. Try sharing a meal and discover what I call the ultimate "meal deal."

Other creative financial findings are all around your home. Throughout the house, the closets, the garage, the shed, and other areas there are likely to be dozens of items that could be sold to generate income.

Two summers ago, my family did this when we started planning how to finance our summer vacation. We discovered we had enough "stuff" to have a garage sale to raise a lot of money.

PROBLEM SOLVING AND DECISION MAKING

After we decided what we were going to do, we sat down and figured out how we were going to do it. The important principle is this: *Never let the problem-solving phase of a plan interfere with the decision-making phase.* If a person had to solve all the problems before making a decision, nothing would ever be decided or get accomplished.

Good managers make decisions based on as much information as they can acquire in a reasonably short period of time. Then they attempt to solve any problems connected with the decision. Every decision has a set of problems. What people really decide when they make a decision is what set of problems they want to work with.

IF ANYTHING IS WORTH DOING, IT'S WORTH DOING WELL

My family had decided to deal with a $2,000 problem created by our decision to take a 6,000 mile summer vacation. It was great fun for our whole family to creatively plan and dream together how we could generate the $2,000. As I mentioned before, we decided to have a garage sale. Now our family didn't "just" have a garage sale. Our garage sale was an event. My parents instilled in me: "If anything is worth doing, it is worth doing well."

If Anything Is Worth Doing, It Is Worth Doing Well

Our signs were very professional looking. We advertised well. We hung colorful flag ropes all over the yard to attract attention. All of our merchandise was carefully handled and clearly marked. Even the location was thoughtfully chosen to provide us with the best possible visibility and accessibility.

We smiled and warmly greeted people when they came. After all, look at what God tells us about how to treat strangers:

"Don't forget to be kind to strangers, for some who have done this have entertained angels without realizing it."
(Hebrews 13:2 Living Bible)

In the garage sale business, I have seen many people planning for failure. They put up small, hastily scribbled signs that are difficult if not impossible to read. They grunt at you when you show up, instead of greeting you. Everything is in disorderly piles. It looks more like a junk sale than a rare jewel sale. With just a little effort, they could sell many items and make good money.

Some other creative funding ideas our family came up with included collecting aluminum cans and newspapers. Our son mowed lawns. Our daughter cleaned homes with a friend. I did some extra speaking engagements and wrote articles for publications. Mary sold some arts and crafts items she'd created.

As we all committed ourselves to working together using all the creative time, talents and treasures God gave to us, we were able to raise the $2,000. The whole project bonded our family much closer together and we enjoyed a rewarding summer vacation.

YOU CAN HAVE BARRELS OF FUN
WITHOUT NEEDING BARRELS OF MONEY

Our creativity was also needed in keeping the trip cost efficient. We checked with our travel agency before we left. They often have insider tips on how to save. We brought along an ice chest filled with pop, fresh fruit, candy bars and other munchies. We looked for gas stations located a few blocks off the main freeway exits with lower gas prices.

I had prepared an itinerary which allowed us to line up some free housing with friends and relatives. We cut food costs by splitting meals. We asked gas station attendants or restaurant personnel for any available coupons for main attractions in the area.

By using some of these simple cost-reducing ideas, *we had barrels of fun without needing barrels of money.*

You Can Have Barrels Of Fun Without Barrels Of Money

VALUABLE VACANCIES

Because we've never had barrels of money, we've been forced to think about ways our family could have an outstanding vacation without going into outstanding debt.

This summer we're doing what we've done during five different summer vacations. I contacted friends in California who were going on vacation and volunteered to house-sit for them. We take care of their home, yard, pets, and plants while they're away. Instead of paying high hotel rates, we provide a service by staying in their home, and we leave a "love gift" to help cover utility costs.

Empty homes have turned into valuable vacancies for us. This may be a good idea for you to pursue as well. Our family loves the ocean, which is why we chose California. You may prefer mountains or wooded areas or large cities. A good place to start your search for a house-sitting opportunity is with a church in your desired area. They can announce your need to their membership or place an ad in their newsletter.

CREATED TO BE CREATIVE

God created us to be creative. The more creative we are, the more creative our lifestyle becomes. It didn't take me long as a young, energetic minister to figure out that the dreams God was giving me for helping all the people God was bringing to Community Church of Joy couldn't be accomplished by using only the Sunday morning offering.

Many people gave generously and sacrificially. However, what was given was only enough to maintain what was already taking place. If Community Church of Joy was going to move ahead, we needed to creatively think about how to move beyond Sunday morning offerings into creative finances.

*Always Make
The Most Of
What You Have*

ALWAYS MAKE THE MOST OF WHAT YOU HAVE

It's essential to make the most of each Sunday morning offering. I highly recommend that every church receiving an offering assign someone to immediately place the money into an interest-bearing account or invest in another safe high interest-bearing instrument first thing each Monday morning. This way you maximize the offering fully until you actually need it to pay necessary obligations. There may be many days that elapse before the money in your account is actually taken out to honor the payment of your checks.

Never let any money sit in safes, drawers, on desk tops, or anyplace else. That's "dead" money. Both professionally and personally, good money managers makes sure that their money is being maximized. Yes, even if it's $5.00, invest it! Have a trusted financial expert help you invest in a way that will most benefit you or your organization.

MANY WAYS TO GENEROUSLY GIVE
EVEN WHEN YOU'RE DEAD

I've had the privilege to know and have as a friend Dr. Lyle Schaller, one of America's best consultants on church growth. Dr. Schaller recently shared with me that there are many ways for average persons to creatively give away their money. Certainly, they can and will give out of their normal weekly income. He pointed out that people also have land, stocks, bonds, savings accounts, and dozens of other assets, as well as estate profiles like wills, trusts, and insurances.

A dynamic, growing church needs to provide as many opportunities for people to give as there are ways to give. Our church has had people give land, houses, antique cars, diamond rings and watches, stocks, bonds, and numerous other kinds of gifts.

There are also some people who are remembering the ministry of the church in their wills. Giving 10% or more in your will to your church and to worthy charities is financially responsible.

It's a way to honor God with every area of your finances. No one will be able to take anything with them when they die, but there are humorous stories of those who have tried.

I was told of one funeral procession with a trailer being pulled behind the hearse. The man who died left instructions to load all his things into a U-Haul and bring it along to the funeral. Of course, the cemetery was as far as it got, and after the burial service, instead of taking his belongings back to the house, the relatives gave them all away.

I heard about another man who left instructions that he wanted to be buried in his brand new Cadillac. When one of the bystanders saw this dead man being lowered into the ground in his fancy new car, he said, "Man, that's really livin'!"

How ridiculous all of this is! The material side of living ends absolutely when death comes. That's why it's so important to make sure your material possessions are invested in something that will be of lasting value.

BEING PREPARED TO DIE PREPARES YOU TO LIVE

The most important issue in life that we need to honestly and openly deal with is our relationship to God through Jesus Christ. If I am not prepared to die, I am really not prepared to live. It is important to do some deep soul searching and ask ourselves right now: "If I were to die today, am I sure that I would be with my loving Lord in heaven?" *CAN* we be so sure? The Bible promises it:

> "If we confess our sins, He is faithful and just and will forgive us our sins and purify us from all unrighteousness."
>
> (I John 1:9 NIV)

All we need to do is bow our head and tell Jesus we're sorry for our sins, that we love Him and want Him to be in charge of every area of our life. Then we thank Him for our new beginning. There is "good news" and good reason for everyone who has done this.

"If anyone is in Christ, he is a new creature; the old has gone, the new has come."

(2 Corinthians 5:17 NIV)

*Being Prepared
To Die
Prepares You To
Live*

When we invite God to be our CEO (Chief Executive Officer), there is a confidence and courage that saturates every cell and fiber of our being. *We are not just different, we are new.* God forgives and forgets. We can move ahead with a new sense of destiny, determination, and delight beginning today and being perfected in heaven with our Lord. I invite you to pray the words of this song:

> *"Dear Jesus, Thou art everything to me,*
> *And everything I own I give to Thee.*
> *My life, my all, but most of all,*
> *Dear Lord, I give myself to Thee."*

Our church mission statement is: "That all may know Jesus Christ, we share His love, with power, inspired by the Holy Spirit." The emphasis is on people coming to Christ. It's no wonder that the people of Joy have chosen every creative means possible to finance our mission and ministry.

CREATIVE MONEY RAISING IDEAS

One of the recent most popular and successful ways to raise money for many organizations is "a-Thons." There are Jog-a-Thons, Walk-a-Thons, Rock-a-Thons, Tel-a-Thons, Bike-a-Thons and dozens more.

Recently, we had a Joy-a-Thon where the whole family could participate. All those choosing to be part of the event got a sponsor sheet to be filled out by people willing to pay so much per lap. Participants could walk, crawl, run, jog, bike, skateboard, or whatever method they chose to get around the high school track. They tried to see how many times they could get around in one hour.

The event was sponsored by our youth ministry and the choir sold pop, hot dogs, candy bars and auctioned pies to raise money for their special projects. Money was raised through this event and the bonus was that everyone had an enjoyable time doing it.

Another creative idea to raise money to help people is to

sponsor major concerts or well-known lecturers. Community Church of Joy has sponsored concerts by Pat and Debby Boone, Noel Paul Stookey, the Imperials, the Blackwood Brothers, Andrus and Blackwood, and many others, plus speaking engagements by Dr. Robert Schuller and John DeLorean.

Every one of these major events brought hundreds of people to our church. Many came with enormous needs and we were able to help them. Hundreds attending one or more of these special events didn't have a home church and so they joined ours. Creative events like these help, both financially and numerically, the future growth of the entire Christian church. Always remember that Christians are on the same team. When one church wins, everybody wins.

Another creative idea for raising money is to plan ahead for something extraordinary at special times of the year. For example, this last Christmas season we ran a program called "A December to Remember." Christmas is a generous giving time of the year. Everyone is buying presents for their loved ones. Well, the one who loves best is God.

This past Christmas, we invited each person to give their greatest Christmas gift to God. People were encouraged to match or exceed their largest gift with a gift to the Lord. We sent invitation letters with specially designed envelopes enclosed. We had weekly announcements during the church service. We publicized the program in our weekly newspaper and through many other channels. Joy raised about $55,000 during this creative Christmas celebration.

Always Keep In Mind Excellence And Enthusiasm

TWO KEY PRINCIPLES

Whenever you're doing creative, special financing programs, it's important to remember a couple of things:

1. Remember the cause must be perceived as very important. For our "December to Remember" campaign, we promised that the money raised would be used to help our youth ministry which involves over 450 teenagers.

We also promised that some of the money would be used to help our children and adult education programs obtain more temporary classrooms. We promised that some of it would be used to complete our beautiful sanctuary.

Finally, we promised to use a portion of the money for staffing needs. As you can see, there was something important for everyone to get excited about.

2. What the money is used for must benefit as many people as possible. That will ensure the greatest possible participation in the project. Be sure your projects are inclusive and not exclusive.

MORE CREATIVE MONEY RAISING IDEAS

For Mother's Day, we usually do something especially creative. To give an extraordinary financial gift of love on Mother's Day is exciting for many people.

The telephone companies tell us that their second busiest day in the entire year is Mother's Day. Christmas is busiest. (I'm told that Father's Day ranks right up there with Halloween and Ground Hog Day.) Extending an invitation to participate in something financially creative on Mother's Day can be a profitable idea.

Another creative financing idea is to have a bookstore on the campus of your church. People need the faith-building influence that Christian books, tapes, art, crafts, and other items provide.

Selling clothes imprinted with your church's or organization's logo can also be a good source of income. There's probably a corner someplace that you can attractively fix up so people will want to browse and buy merchandise.

We raise a few thousand dollars each year by sponsoring a golf tournament. Many people who play golf have a lot of fun playing in these events. You could sponsor a tennis tournament, a bowling tournament, a softball tournament, a horseshoe tournament, or any other kind of tournament you can dream up. *Creative financing can and should be a lot of fun.*

Think Beyond Your Present Thoughts

THINK BEYOND YOUR PRESENT THOUGHTS

I encourage you never to limit your territory. There are people in the community all around you who may not belong to your church or organization who would enjoy participating in and supporting your creative financing program. Look beyond your membership lists. Think beyond your present thoughts about who your contacts are. People are the greatest resource. New and creative events and ideas get people excited.

You will need to think beyond your own likes or dislikes and interests. An event like a golf tournament may not appeal to you because you don't play the game. However, there are thousands of people out there who would fly across the country to participate in a well-organized, well-executed golf tournament.

CREATIVITY HELPS YOU GROW STRONGER AND WISER

The first time you try a creative idea, you may not have hundreds respond. Don't give up. Don't quit. Use each creative event as a building block. Every time you'll get stronger, wiser, and you'll receive greater financial reward.

Creativity Helps You Grow Stronger And Wiser

CONCERNING EXCELLENCE AND ENTHUSIASM

One final word of caution. When we plan, organize, and execute our creative God-given, God-inspired ideas, we need to be sure that every detail of the event itself is executed as enthusiastically as the original idea. In other words, the best results are achieved when we do things "first class."

Printed materials need to project an image of creativity and excitement. The event itself needs to be filled with expectation, inspiration, and surprise. When that happens, people will look forward to doing it again. Those who supported you the first time need to leave with the eagerness of wanting to be a part of the event again next time.

Sometimes Christian churches, charitable organizations, and other well-meaning people are sloppy with planning, publicity, and the event follow-through. The thinking seems to be, "Let's throw something together and see if it works." I assure you it doesn't.

We're the "King's kids." We're part of a royal family. We are caring for priceless, precious people. An image of beauty and excellence needs to be communicated. God and God's people deserve the best—never second best. The Bible makes this clear in Colossians 3:23 (NIV):

> *"Whatever you do, work at it with all your heart, as working for the Lord, not for men."*

*Success Is
Helping People
Become The
Best They Can
Possibly Be*

HELP PEOPLE BECOME
THE BEST THEY CAN POSSIBLY BE

As a Christian, I believe that Jesus Christ is the best product in the world to market. I continually ask God to give me all the creativity possible so that people everywhere will come to understand that God loves them unconditionally and non-judgmentally. God wants to be their friend. The Lord can help them become the best they can possibly be.

Before we move on, I invite you to ponder these questions:

1. What are my financial obstacles right now (both personally and professionally)?
2. How can I creatively turn my financial obstacles into opportunities?

TURNING FINANCIAL OBSTACLES INTO OPPORTUNITIES

IMPORTANT QUESTIONS

What kind of attitude do you have about money?

Do you think about money or the lack of it during most of your waking hours?

How would you like your attitude to be about money?

WHAT TO DO WITH YOUR CONTROL CENTER

Our thoughts and feelings about money can be made fresh and new. Let me tell you how. One of the most important centers of our being is the "interbrain." The interbrain controls the nervous center which keeps the heart, stomach, and lungs functioning harmoniously. The interbrain, which includes the thalamus and hypothalamus, is also the governor of emotions, such as love, hate, fear, etc.

Medical doctors inform us that ulcers of the stomach, palpitations of the heart, and other types of inner emotional storms originate in the interbrain. This interbrain is just below the forebrain or cerebrum which takes up most of the area within the skull.

The forebrain helps us to analyze, think, and make decisions, and to process other information. The interbrain then takes that information and those thoughts and reports to the rest of our body how we should feel about what is happening.

For example, let's suppose that you've received a letter from the bank telling you that your account is overdrawn. A negative response to this information, received by the forebrain and intercepted by the interbrain, would stir up a real "emotional storm."

On the other hand, a positive response received by the forebrain and intercepted by the interbrain, would tend to generate a "rise above the situation" response.

I believe that the key to having a fresh, new, positive attitude is to commit our interbrain and forebrain to Jesus Christ. Let Him take charge of our "control center." When Christ is in charge of our emotionally responsive inner being, we can enjoy genuine health and happiness in every arena of our lives, including our finances. Because money can be such an emotional issue, it's essential that we look to Christ to shape and control both our attitudes and our actions in all of our money matters.

A Person Can Give Money Without Loving God, But A Person Cannot Love God Without Giving Money

"LOOKING GOOD" OR "LOVING GOD"

Every time I give a message or lecture on the topic of money, I issue this challenge concerning our attitude about it:
A person can give their money without loving God, but a person cannot love God without giving their money.

It's respectable and even prestigious to give money away. Some people are able to satisfy their conscience by sometimes giving money to needy causes. However, when we move beyond "looking good" to "loving God," that's another matter. Out of a God-shaped heart flows generosity and a genuine giving spirit.

HARD QUESTIONS NEED HONEST ANSWERS

In helping ourselves develop a positive, healthy attitude toward finances, let's take a look at our own honest answers to these five questions:

1. Am I willing to acknowledge that God owns everything?
2. Do I have an attitude of gratitude?
3. How generous am I?
4. How sacrificial am I willing to be?
5. What am I investing in that will have lasting value?

When I answered these key questions, I discovered what my real financial obstacles were and how I could change those obstacles into opportunities. These five questions uncover for us that which is of priceless value.

1. *AM I WILLING TO ACKNOWLEDGE THAT GOD OWNS EVERYTHING?*

This gets at the heart of unhealthy pride and arrogance. Tiny tots on up to grown adults sometimes cry out, "That's mine!" The "mine-ism mentality" is destructive and leads to greed. Greed leads a person to falsely assume that genuine success is measured by the accumulation of things. Greedy persons think that the more "stuff" they can claim belongs to them, the higher their status is elevated.

Everything Belongs To God

If we are being honest, we must acknowledge that everything we have is a gift from God. I like the words to a song I used to sing every Sunday morning in church as I was growing up:

> *"We give Thee but Thine own,*
> *What e'er the gift may be.*
> *All that we have is Thine alone,*
> *A trust, O Lord, from Thee."*

God has entrusted us with everything we have. When we brag, we should brag about God and the fact that we've been allowed to borrow for a few short years all of the possessions we have. With that kind of positive attitude, we can freely celebrate and enjoy life, because the possessions we have will not possess us. Even if we were to lose everything, we wouldn't collapse because we realize that our possessions never were ours to begin with and they never will be. Everything belongs to God.

Remember the story about Joe and the fire that destroyed his automotive business? Joe's positive response to his terrible loss was to say, "Pastor Walt, my business belongs to the Lord. It isn't mine. God allowed the fire to come, and God will take care of everything that needs to be taken care of."

The essential ingredient to Joe's calm response was that he'd acknowledged that God owned everything, including his business. Joe was free from being consumed by fires of rage or resentment because he was only the manager. God was the owner. Here's what the Bible says:

> *"Everything under heaven belongs to me (God)."*
> (Job 41:11b NIV)

*There Is No Way
You Can Lose In
Being Generous*

I'm reminded of a story about a little boy named Robert who got his hand stuck in a cookie jar. His mom and dad tried desperately to free his little hand. Finally, they realized that the reason he couldn't pull it out was because he had his fist clinched.

So, Mom and Dad told little Robert to open up his hand and he could easily pull it out. Robert refused. Tearfully he said, "If I open my hand, I'll lose the penny I found in the bottom of the jar."

We've all heard of people who cling so tightly to money that they are said to make it squeak. Others are called tightwads. God created us to live free from being possessed by our possessions. In fact, only the things that we cling to so tightly can destroy us.

Whatever we place in God's hands and bring before God with our open hands and open hearts will be bountifully blessed for God's glory and our good. Martin Luther once said, "I have tried to keep things in my own hands and have lost them all. But what I have given into God's hands...that I still possess."

I invite you to join me right now in praying:

"Thank you, Lord, for everything I have is a gift from you. I humbly acknowledge that you own everything including my home, my business, my car and all of my other possessions."

Join me in singing this little Gospel chorus:

Dear Jesus, Thou art everything to me -
And everything I own I give to Thee;
My wealth, my all, but most of all,
Dear Lord, I give myself to Thee.

Is My Money Preparing Hearts For Heaven?

2. "DO I HAVE AN ATTITUDE OF GRATITUDE?"

We all know people who are never happy. It seems that nothing satisfies them. You never hear them giving thanks for what they have. They're always complaining about what they don't have. If you ask them how things are going, they always respond, "It could be better." These kinds of people buy a new house and when they talk about it, they can't wait to tell you everything that's wrong with it.

The Bible is very clear concerning this whole area of gratitude and thankful living. In I Thessalonians, the fifth chapter, verse 18, it says:

> "Give thanks in all circumstances, for this is God's will for you in Jesus Christ."

Also, the Psalmist tells us to:

> "Give thanks to the Lord, for he is good."
>
> (Psalm 136:1 NIV)

A grateful heart helps us get the most joy, the most satisfaction, the most delight, and the most enjoyment out of what we have, no matter how much or how little it may be. The happiest people in the world are not necessarily the people with the most money or the best cars or the biggest houses. The happiest people are those with the most thankful hearts and the best attitudes of gratitude.

A person whose life demonstrates this clearly is Mother Teresa of Calcutta. She has no material possessions, yet her life is what she describes as sheer joy. She works with the poorest of the poor. She sees thousands of them die with joy on their lips and hearts filled with thanksgiving, largely because she continually spreads her attitude of gratitude.

3. HOW GENEROUS AM I?

This question needs our undivided attention now. Here's "good news" directly from the Bible concerning generosity:

"Good will come to him who is generous..."
(Psalm 112:5a NIV)

"A generous man will prosper; he who refreshes others will himself be refreshed."
(Proverbs 11:25 NIV)

Psychologists tell us that generous people live healthier and happier lives. God created us to be generous, giving people.

"God so loved the world that He gave His only Son, that whoever believes in Him will not perish but have everlasting life."
(John 3:16 NIV)

Here's how it works:

"Remember this: Whoever sows sparingly will also reap sparingly, and whoever sows generously will also reap generously."
(II Corinthians 9:6 NIV)

A Sacrificial Gift Exceeds A Convenient Gift

There is no way you can lose by being generous. Generosity honors God. Generous people are a delight to be with. And generosity is contagious—it breeds generosity.

My dad is a very generous person. As a result, our whole family has become generous. In other cases where a parent is stingy, the family takes on this characteristic and finds it difficult, if not impossible, to give generously.

I encourage you to take the lead in being generous. See if you can outdo one another in generosity. That way God wins, you win, and everybody else wins!

4. "HOW SACRIFICIAL AM I WILLING TO BE?"

This question is enormously difficult to deal with. Sacrifice requires deep commitment. The Bible encourages this in Ephesians 5:1-2 NIV:

> "Be imitators of God, therefore, as dearly loved children and live a life of love, just as Christ loved us and gave Himself up for us as a fragrant offering and sacrifice to God."

I recently learned a lot about sacrifice from a nurse who was one of those sacrificially committed people I'd long pictured in my mind. Dottie, a young mother, had been on life support systems for over three days following a massive aneurism explosion in her brain. When the final brain activity test had been taken, it was confirmed that Dottie was brain dead. After the family received the awful news, they agreed together with the doctor to remove all life support systems.

Dottie's nurse removed all the systems. Then she immediately knelt down beside Dot's bed, grabbing her hand and holding it tightly until the monitor indicated a flat line on all her vital signs.

As this loving servant let go of Dottie's lifeless hand, I asked why she cared so completely for her patients. Her reply was beautiful. "I AM COMMITTED TO LOVING PEOPLE," she said.

Success Is Being Committed To Loving People

This same nurse shared with me that only a few months earlier, her teenage son had shot himself in the head. She'd gone through a similar deathbed experience with him. Her commitment to loving and caring for people transcended any normal expectation of giving. Overcoming bitterness and resentment that she may have harbored over the tragic loss of her only son required enormous sacrifice, and she kept right on loving and giving sacrificially of herself.

It takes commitment to be a sacrificial person. Commitment, as I mentioned earlier, is more than a feeling. It's a decision. Commitment is a banking term for deposit. When we deposit all of our assets—our time, our talent, and our treasures—in God's bank, those assets become stronger and more secure.

Jesus Christ insured our strength and security by sacrificing Himself on a cross. All that He has done and is doing guarantees an extraordinary return on our life's investment. When we consider God's great sacrifice of Christ, any financial sacrifice we might make seems quite small.

A sacrificial gift exceeds a convenient gift. Convenience doesn't really change our lifestyle much. On the other hand, sacrifice radically changes our lifestyle.

When my wife, Mary, and I increased our giving from 10% to 20% of our income, we realized that our style of living would have to change. Some of the things that were nice and comfortable had to be sacrificed in order to keep our 20% commitment.

I'm sure that as we move closer to our goal of giving 50% of our income away, it will require an even greater sacrifice than we are experiencing today. Yet, I realize that giving 50% of our income away is perhaps less of a sacrifice than a person in a third world country giving away 10% of their income. God calls us not to equal gifts, but to equal sacrifice.

5. "WHAT AM I INVESTING IN THAT WILL LAST?"

This may be the most difficult question to answer honestly. Another way to put the question would be: Is what I am using my money for preparing hearts for heaven? Will my money be used to help people discover the "good news" of Christ's unconditional love and unlimited grace so that they can live in heaven forever with God?

Smart money managers look for the very best investment possible. They want to make sure that their money is doing all that it can. Money invested in meaningful ministry where people are being helped in the name of Jesus Christ is a "premium," "blue chip" investment.

Let's talk straight here. Investments in cars or houses or boats or golf club memberships or hunting trips or vacations or jewelry or other "things" are all temporal. In other words, all of these things are nice and certainly there is nothing wrong with investing in them. But they're all valueless, eternally speaking.

You and I work hard for our money. Our money needs to do the most good for the most people. To know that through the money I've invested in meaningful ministry, another person will live with Jesus Christ forever is completely satisfying and gratifying, too. All my efforts can really pay high dividends. With God's help, the more I earn, the more I have to invest in eternity. That's the greatest financial incentive program going today!

WHY DO WE HAVE MONEY?

It's so easy to forget why we have all the money we have. Television advertisements lure us into thinking the purpose of our money is for traveling to places and using it for our own gratification here and now. Newspaper ads lead us to think that our money is for buying the things they're selling which will then bring us happiness. Radio jingles try to convince us that our money can buy us companionship and friendship in a club or resort-like community.

Money will never do for people what only God can. There are people who are miserable throughout their entire life because they have never discovered this truth. The Bible tells it pretty straight:

> *"I am the way, the truth, and the life. No one comes to the Father except through Me."*
>
> (John 14:7 NIV)

Jesus is the way home. Jesus is the way to happiness. Jesus is the only way to turning financial obstacles into financial opportunities.

THE TRUTH ABOUT LIFE, DEATH AND LIFE AFTER DEATH

Jesus is the only truth about life, about death, and about life after death. That's great stuff! It's pretty simple and yet, sometimes, it's awfully tough to come to grips with. My purpose in writing this book would be accomplished if readers who don't know Jesus Christ as their personal Lord and Savior would receive Jesus Christ into their lives.

I encourage you to dedicate as much as you have discovered to be true about you in these past chapters to as much as you've discovered to be true about Jesus Christ. You see, the Christian life is dynamic, not static. Once you make the commitment, you will either grow closer to the Lord or further away. Through regular prayer, worship, Bible study, and spending time with other Christian people, you will grow healthier and happier in your Christian pilgrimage.

Money Will Never Do For People What Only God Can Do

JESUS ONLY, NOT JESUS AND...

The bottom line is really this: Jesus only—not Jesus and everything else. ONLY JESUS CHRIST CAN HELP YOU TURN YOUR FINANCIAL OBSTACLES INTO OPPORTUNITIES. With Him managing your money, your finances absolutely have unlimited possibilities.

There will be financially tough times. There will be financial storms and struggles. However, the key to financial success is to keep your eyes on Jesus. He can and will help you manage your money without losing your mind. I love the old Gospel song:

"Turn you eyes upon Jesus.
Look full in His wonderful face,
And the things of earth will grow strangely dim,
In the light of His glory and grace."

Each chapter in this book has made it clear that life is filled with financial obstacles. Even as I wrote these words, I received an emergency phone call from a remarkably gifted person who is facing the worst financial obstacle of his life. His first response was panic. He looked for an easy way out. The more he studied his problem, the more he wanted to take the path of least resistance. I encouraged him not to run away or ignore the crisis or do anything that would complicate the problem further. He needed to face the obstacle and turn it into an opportunity with God's help.

FINANCIAL OBSTACLES

Financial obstacles that may emerge can come from countless sources:

    a.   start-up costs of a new business
    b.   sudden, uncontrollable growth
    c.   money management mistakes
    d.   the lack of good financial planning

e. poor budgeting establishment and implementation
f. lack of vision
g. not properly meeting the needs of people
h. too much debt to service
i. restricted cash flow
j. the absence of generosity
k. inadequate marketing skills
l. an attitude needing positive adjustment
m. unwillingness to sacrifice
n. unwillingness to ask for help
o. wants exceeding needs
p. leaving God out of the picture
q. unmet staffing needs or over-staffing
r. absence of clearly defined goals
s. unwillingness to risk
t. communication problems
u. dishonesty
v. not establishing an enthusiastic climate
w. the need for more staying power or "stick-to-it-iveness"
x. more creativity and innovation needed
y. inadequate commitment to excellence
z. a need to put life's priorities in proper order

FINANCIAL OPPORTUNITIES

That was an alphabet full of obstacles and there are plenty more. However, the key to overcoming financial obstacles is not to focus on the obstacle, but on the opportunity. Let's take each obstacle and, with God's help, transform it into a financial opportunity:

a. Starting a new business will give you more earning *opportunity* than ever before.
b. Growth can bring with it more healthy *opportunities*.
c. Learning from money management mistakes gives one an *opportunity* to become a better person.
d. Learning how to do effective financial planning opens windows of *opportunity*.

e. Developing and living on a budget gives a person the *opportunity* to become financially stronger and more stable.
f. Great vision always inspires great *opportunity*.
g. When people's needs are met, *opportunity* keeps knocking at the door.
h. Becoming debt-free promotes the freedom to take advantage of new *opportunities*.
i. Improving cash flow creates a new *opportunity* to confidently move ahead.
j. Generosity is pregnant with *opportunity*.
k. Marketing well is a key to providing widespread *opportunity*.
l. A positive attitude attracts *opportunity*.
m. Sacrifice is the beginning of *opportunity*.
n. Willingness to ask for help strengthens *opportunity*.
o. Keeping needs ahead of wants is essential for *opportunity*.
p. With God, everything is an outstanding *opportunity*.
q. A cared-for staff is a caring staff eager to join in on *opportunity*.
r. Set high goals and you're set for high *opportunity*.
s. Risk is the essence of faith that fuels *opportunity*.
t. Communication is the nerve center of *opportunity*.
u. Honesty establishes the ground rules for *opportunity*.
v. Enthusiasm is the heart of *opportunity*.
w. Staying power is the launching pad for *opportunity*.
x. Creativity is the best friend of *opportunity*.
y. A commitment to excellence is a generator for *opportunity*.
z. Prioritizing life makes the most out of every *opportunity*.

This past summer during my visit to Communist China, I was told by our tour guide that the same symbol used in the Chinese word for "obstacle" was also used for "opportunity." It was left to the persons using the word how they chose to interpret it. The transliteration of the Chinese character or symbols form the word "wuijee" ("wui" meaning risk or danger, and "jee" meaning opportunity). How will I choose to interpret the word today?

We can choose to focus on the obstacles of finances or we can choose to focus on the opportunities inherent in every financial obstacle. The decision we make now will determine our destiny.

I pray that each of us will choose opportunity. Then we'll most assuredly meet one day and claim our ultimate prize together.

*Out Of
A God Shaped
Heart
Flows
Generosity*

HOW TO DEVELOP AND IMPLEMENT A SUCCESSFUL FINANCIAL PROGRAM

A provocative newspaper columnist, Ginger Hutton of the ARIZONA REPUBLIC, wrote about her struggle with finances. She said: "Two money issues have been on my mind lately: one is church donations, the other is tipping."

Over the years, I've heard people complain about having to tip in restaurants. My sympathies have been on the side of waiters or waitresses ever since my daughter waited tables for awhile. I saw how hard she worked for her tips and how much she depended on them to supplement her modest wages.

Tipping is an excellent example of free enterprise at work. The customer rewards the waiter or waitress according to how the job is performed.

I used to dutifully figure out an exact 15 percent on each bill, until one day I realized I was quibbling over whether or not to leave an extra quarter. A quarter wasn't going to affect me much one way or the other, but 25 cents more from each customer during the day could make a real difference for a financially struggling young man or woman.

If the tip were included in the price of the food and the servers were paid a standard wage, dinner prices would go up and the incentive to provide extra service would vanish.

The 15 to 20 percent rule also makes it financially fair to the customer. If you can only afford to eat at an inexpensive restaurant, then your tip is smaller. If you can afford a $100 food bill, you can afford a $15 to $20 tip.

Another place where we hate to let go of our money is in church. It continues to surprise me that some people give only a dollar or so each week to the church as they did years ago, even though costs for everything else have quadrupled. Yet these same people think nothing about spending $5 for a movie ticket, for instance, or of paying several times that amount for dinner and a concert, but still will drop change or single bills into the collection plate.

It occurs to me that some church members must think the church is supported directly by God. Perhaps they believe a series of miracles produces money for charity and missionary work, minister's salary, organist's fees, air conditioning, school bus tires, printed church bulletins, and new paint on the steeple. I've observed, however, that God often works such miracles through people and their pocketbooks.

I admit that I've been uncomfortable when asked for money in church. I examined that discomfort and finally realized that board members aren't asking me to donate to the building fund so they can pocket the money. They're putting a lot of work and time into asking me and others to help support something we love.

When I give to the church, I'm not only giving to help others, I'm giving to myself. I wonder why it took me so long to figure that out? What kind of program can be developed to help us figure out how to become more giving to ourselves and to others? Practically speaking, what works?

Begin putting together a financial program that works by putting together a team of champions. People with winning attitudes attract winners. It's fun to be part of a winning team, even though it means a lot of hard work.

PLAY TO WIN

I'll always remember the comment made by Rollie Massemino, the head coach of Villanova, when his team was about to play the Hoyas of Georgetown. Rollie had been to church the morning before that game and had this inspiring thought. During the pre-game pep talk, he told his players, "Gentleman, I want you to go out there today and play to win, instead of playing not to lose."

We Don't Have It
All Together
But Together We
Have It All

What a profound challenge! How many people begin each day, or face great challenges, with the idea of simply trying not to lose? People try not to lose the sale....or they try not to lose their job...or they try not to lose their marriage. People who win go out each day expecting to make that sale...expecting to excel at their job...deciding to strengthen their marriage.

That's how we faced our church's finances, and that's my attitude toward dealing with my personal finances. I maintain the idea that great financial developments come from decisions to make good financial plans. Positive, expectant planning produces positive results.

I put together a strong team of champions to develop a program that would strengthen our church's finances. Our congregation was moving forward in a positive fashion and I wanted to bring as much encouragement and enthusiasm to the people of Joy as I possibly could. So together we developed a program to really help people.

One by one I met with each person who was chosen and extended a personal invitation to them to become part of this winning team. I was honest about the great demands and rewards of this mission. We prayed together, and when they said yes, we made a covenant that no matter what it took in terms of time, energy, or resources, we would do it together. We don't have it all together, but together we have it all.

*Play To Win
Instead Of
Playing Not To
Lose*

FIVE WINNING QUALITIES OF A CHAMPION

Every successful financial program needs strong leaders who are genuine champions. When I look for a champion who has a winning attitude, I look for five essential qualities. With these qualities, I believe the result can be genuine success far beyond our greatest dreams or expectations.

Number One: A great champion has made a commitment to worship the Lord regularly—that is, acknowledging that God is in charge. It's a time to let God inspire, renew, refresh, and fill us up with enthusiasm. (Enthusiasm means to be full of God.) Worshiping each week also keeps us tuned in to Gods's wavelength.

Number Two: A great champion has made a commitment to daily prayer and Bible reading. Praying is letting God in on everything we're doing. It's a chance for us to get the right signals directly from the head coach. It's much more purposeful and fruitful to live life in God's power than on our own. Bible reading lets God love us through love letters. Reading the Bible is a direct communication memo from the Chairman of the Board on how to conduct our business affairs.

Number Three: A great champion has made a commitment to grow mentally, emotionally, physically, and spiritually. Champions are committed to being the best they can possibly be. They are willing to attend continuing education courses dealing with every dimension of life. They are willing to read and expand through knowledge. They are willing to eat right, get enough sleep, and exercise regularly. They are also willing to get involved in continuing Christian education courses.

People With Winning Attitudes Attract Winners

Number Four: A great champion has made a commitment to tithing. That means giving at least the first 10% of one's income to the Lord through the church or another dynamic Christian organization. Tithing is saying that God is #1 in our lives and that God is the most important part of everything we have, all that we are, and who we hope to become. Until persons are willing to tithe, they aren't compassionately generous. Certainly, people who don't tithe can be wonderful, but they're not compassionately generous people. The Bible explains it this way:

> *"One man gives freely, yet gains even more; another*
> *withholds unduly, but comes to poverty. A generous*
> *man will prosper; he who refreshes others will himself*
> *be refreshed."*
>
> (Proverbs 11:24-25 NIV)

Number Five: A great champion had made a commitment to being reproductive. It's not as important to be productive as it is to be reproductive. We can do a lot of great things, but helping other people to become successful, responsible, and to become winners, too, is the true sign of greatness.

The Best Is Yet To Be

SUCCESSFUL FINANCIAL ADVANCEMENT
PROGRAM DETAILS

After the champions are in place, they receive some simple job descriptions that are helpful in the management of recruited champion volunteers. Here are some examples:

1. TAKING CHARGE

THE PASTORAL STAFF. I believe that pastors need to lead their people. A church without strong pastoral leadership flounders. Great churches have pastors who provide positive, enthusiastic, dynamic leadership. If the pastor is excited and committed to something, the people will also be excited and committed.

I'm not suggesting that the pastor do all the work, but the pastor needs to encourage, build up, compliment, train, motivate and deploy leadership. I attended every meeting of our financial advancement program because I never ask people to do anything I myself am not willing to so. A successful financial advancement program starts with the pastor or pastors.

2. MAKING SURE IT GETS DONE

THE CHAIRPEOPLE. The chairpeople make sure everyone follows through on their assigned jobs. They chair all the meetings. They are responsible for training, recruiting, and motivating directors and their committees. This group serves as the liaison among the pastors, directors, and congregation. They're the ones who make sure the jobs get done.

3. A MULTI-MEDIA PRODUCTION

THE MULTI-MEDIA DIRECTORS. These people assemble the greatest possible multi-media presentation for the congregational banquet which is the culmination of the financial advancement program. (NOTE: We held this banquet on Palm Sunday evening, one of the best nights of the year for a celebration banquet.)

This group is instructed to include as many pictures as possible of members and close friends of the church in the multi-media presentation. When people see themselves, a family member, or a close friend on a large screen, they feel like a significant part of the entire organization. Every department and program of the church needs to be included. People like to see that they're part of something really great.

4. A THANKSGIVING DINNER

THE BANQUET DIRECTORS. This group is responsible for the banquet to celebrate the wonderful ministry and God's cherished people. It's especially a time of tremendous thanksgiving for all the wonderful things God has done and will continue to do.

These directors find a location, select the menu, negotiate prices, coordinate seating and table arrangements, ensure the decorations are properly placed, and they're responsible for clean-up.

5. GETTING THE "GOOD NEWS" OUT

THE PUBLICITY DIRECTORS. Publicity is the key to any successful program. It's impossible to over-advertise or over-publicize. We announce an event a minimum of four weeks in a row in order to reach the majority of our people. Every week we do something more creative and innovative in our publicity than the week before.

The publicity directors are in charge of getting all the information of this financial advancement campaign into our weekly newspaper. They are to coordinate the making of banners, brochures, invitations, and posters. They are to be as innovative and creative as possible.

6. RAISING PEOPLE

THE SMALL GROUP CARE AND SHARE DIRECTORS. It's true that *"people don't care how much you know, until they know how much you care."* A superior financial advancement program is not only designed to raise more money, it's designed to raise people.

This group of directors is asked to design small group caring and sharing Bible studies and rap sessions that will raise people's confidence. They are instructed to offer these groups every day of the week for four weeks, including morning, afternoon, and evening sessions. It's assigned to these directors to find the right inspiring materials or to write their own.

Each week deals with one of the six areas of confidence building: Week 1: Worship; Week 2: Prayer and Devotional Life; Week 3: Bible Study/Christian Growth; Week 4: Witnessing; Week 5: Small Group Fellowship; and Week 6: Tithing. The goal is to have as many members as possible attending at least one session per week.

7. COMMITMENT

THE COMMITMENT CARD DIRECTORS: Every Sunday morning during the six weeks of the actual congregational phase of the program, the people are asked to make a commitment. A special commitment card for each area is to be designed—one for Worship, one for Prayer and Devotional Life, one for Bible Study/Christian Growth, one for Witnessing, one for Small Group Fellowship, and one for Tithing.

Each week after they are signed, these cards are placed on the altar by worshipers wishing to make a commitment to one of these areas. A confidence-building message by a pastor is given to explain each area of the Christian walk. Then an invitation for commitment is extended. Those who make a commitment are encouraged by receiving an attractively designed button saying, "I Am Committed." After each card is signed, it is collected. Then every name is printed in our weekly publication. This lets our entire congregation know something great is happening to a lot of special people.

8. REACH OUT AND TOUCH SOMEONE

THE TELEPHONE CALLING DIRECTORS: Telephone calling is an art. Some people are very good on the telephone and others are not. I've found that some of the best telephone personalities are people in sales. People who make their living over the telephone do extremely well in calling to invite every member to all of the special events—especially the celebration banquet.

The directors in charge of this area are to recruit, train, and motivate all the callers, obtain membership lists, and make assignments. Also, they are to develop a good follow-up program to ensure that everyone is contacted.

9. CREATING A POSITIVE CLIMATE

THE HOSTS AND HOSTESS DIRECTORS: Creating a warm, loving, friendly climate is essential to any successful work, ministry or program. Every gathering needs to have people welcome those attending with a beautiful smile and a friendly handshake or hug. The directors responsible for the hosts and hostesses hold training sessions on how to be especially friendly welcomers. They actually practice hugging and welcoming one another. When I attended the celebration dinner, I was hugged about a hundred times. It was great!

Other responsibilities for these directors include getting escorts to bring people to the banquet tables, getting car parking attendants, and providing refreshments for the planning meetings of all the directors. Then they follow all this up by sending thank you letters to all the champion helpers in the program.

Communication
Is The Key To
Excellence

10. COMMUNICATION

THE INTER-COMMITTEE COMMUNICATION DIREC-
TORS: I love the story about the florist who received phone calls
from two different people wanting to place orders for floral arrangements to be sent for two distinctly different, but very special, occasions.

The first order came in for flowers to be sent to a family
whose grandfather had suddenly died. The second order came
for a young couple celebrating their second wedding anniversary
by moving to a new part of the country.

The florist got the two orders mixed up. The first one was
delivered to the family grieving the loss of a loved one, with a little
card attached to the flowers which read, "Good luck in your new
location." The young couple received the other delivery of
flowers with the message, "We extend our deepest sympathy to
you."

Communication is the key to excellence. The directors in
charge of inter-committee communication are responsible for
channeling information to every directors' group, to the pastors,
to the chairpeople and to the advisory committee. The minutes
of each meeting are compiled and distributed. All upcoming
meetings and important events are communicated. This group
of directors serves as the communications nerve center of the entire operation.

*We Find What
We Look For...
If We Look For
The Good, We
Will Always
Find It*

11. WELCOME HOME

THE OPEN HOUSE DIRECTORS: Throughout a four-month period of time, beginning two months before the actual congregational involvement in the stewardship program, each pastor on staff has an open house each week for a maximum of 30 family units. These open houses are held on Sunday afternoons from 2:00 to 4:00 p.m. Coffee, punch, and cookies are served.

As everyone enters the home, they are asked to sign in and fill out a name tag. Then they get some refreshments. After everyone has arrived, the first 30-40 minutes are spent just getting acquainted. The host pastor then asks each person to tell something about themselves as well as what first attracted them to the church. All of this helps to build stronger friendships and fan the flames of joy and enthusiasm.

12. THE ADVANTAGE OF GOOD ADVICE

THE ADVISORY DIRECTORS: The advisory directors are people in leadership positions within the congregation who give feedback on how they perceive the program to be running. They talk to members of the church to find out how they're responding to the program and pass this information on to all of the directors. Any needed adjustments are then made. These advisors fill in the gaps when an area is experiencing some difficulty in accomplishing its assignment.

THERE IS NO PERFECT CHURCH

It's predictable that after being a member of any church for a period of time, we start seeing the weaknesses of the pastor and the people. We become disillusioned when we discover that the pastor and the members of that Christian church are not perfect. It's at this point that some people start looking around for another church.

After being in over 1,000 different churches all over the world, I can lovingly say I haven't found a perfect church. I'm sure you know why. The organization of the church is run by imperfect people and pastors who sin and make mistakes. The grass is never greener in another church. My encouragement to all is to look for the best where we are and we'll find it.

REMEMBERING WHEN YOU FIRST FELL IN LOVE

I think it's important for church members to be continuously reminded of the great people, programs, and other things that attracted them to becoming a member in the first place. We'll find what we look for. Always remember, the congregation isn't perfect. Only Christ, who gave the gift of the church, is!

We all need to ask ourselves questions like:

1. What would I like to see happen in my church?
2. What do I think could be offered that would make the church stronger, healthier, and more dynamic?
3. How can I help the church serve me and my loved ones in a better way?

SOME MEETING DETAILS

Directors all have a copy of their job descriptions and are accountable to the chairpeople. A report from each director is given at every directors' meeting, held each Tuesday night for four consecutive months.

One of the first orders of business is to make sure everyone understands the vision for the mission. Each person needs to become familiar with the case-statement that articulates the specific, special needs. This is an essential part of the program.

This particular case-statement came to me one morning as I was jogging. I thought about the necessity of meeting the deep needs of people. The hurts, broken lives, and fractured relationships need to be healed. The problems in peoples' lives need to be solved.

I wondered how each of God's people could catch the passion for mission that is needed to become great people and a great church. Then this idea jumped out at me: "We're called from convenience to commitment."

"That's it!" I yelled out loud. Commitment is the key. Nothing significant ever happens without commitment— commitment to the Lord and commitment to one another.

At our next staff meeting, I tested the theme "Called from Convenience to Commitment." The staff liked it. These words captured the essence of what we needed to do. Many people seek convenience. Whatever pleases us and whatever can be done with the least effort is what we often do. We need to call people to a life of excellence...a life of genuine life-transforming, energy-producing commitment, because *high commitment generates high quality.*

The areas that we needed to target for a committed life filled with joy and vitality were:

A. Regular worship attendance
B. Daily prayer and devotions
C. Dynamic Bible study growth groups
D. Small groups of caring and sharing
E. Witnessing and sharing "good news"
F. Tithing

It was evident to every participant in this program that these dynamic qualities really do build people. These commitments help us become the best we can possibly be, mentally, emotionally, physically, and spiritually.

The financial program never was developed to raise a lot of money. It was designed and developed to help people become what God dreamed they would become when they were first created. As it turned out, people were raised, and as a side benefit, a lot of money was raised as well. After this program was completed, the general budget giving increased immediately by more than 20%.